FOR THE GOD OF SMALL CHILDREN:
THE HEART AND HANDS OF A PUPPETEER
A Memoir

FOR THE GOD OF SMALL CHILDREN:
THE HEART AND HANDS OF A PUPPETEER
A Memoir

Don Wallis

The Hutton Street Press
San Luis Obispo, California
2015

First Printing: December 2015

ISBN: 978-0-692-60596-7

The Hutton Street Press
Mission Station
Post Office Box 15552
San Luis Obispo, CA 93406

Website: www.donwallis.com
Email: don@donwallis.com

This memoir is dedicated
to all the children and adults in the world

A List Of Puppet Plays:

Don Quixote
Red Riding Hood
Beauty & The Beast
The Naughty Naughty
Punch & Judy
Hansel & Gretel
Chief Seattle
The Rainbow Bridge
Mark Twain & The White Buffalo
Doc Frog

And a dozen sketches:
shorter plays for special occasions

Also by Don Wallis:
THE PUPPET MAN
New & Selected Poems
The Hutton Street Press, 2014

ACKNOWLEDGEMENTS

I thank Einar Berg, Russell Bunge, Polly Cooper, Mike Cowdrey, Lynne Landweir, James Royer, Dian Sousa and Jesse Stanley for reading this memoir in its earlier drafts and for their kind responses; and I also thank Nancy Abbott, Dennis Anderson, Lee BeDell, Joe Caesar, Dan Canney, Ray Clark Dickson, Marysia Maziarz Dickson, Robert Fritz Folkerts, Ken Hall, Steve Hanson, Jim Henson, Marvin Lee, Richard Levy, Rena Lewis, Glenna Luschei, Michael Malkin, Jack McBade, Dr. Middleton, Mothers For Peace, The Nipomo Swap Meet, Jim & Roberta Owen, Bob Potter, Ed Schum, Steve Smith, David Stacey, Teatro de La Esperanza, Teatro de Los Campesinos, The San Francisco Mime Troupe, The SLO County Health Department, The SLO Downtown Thursday Night Farmers Market, The State of California, The State Parks of California, The Van Beurden Family, Burr Tillstrom & Kukla, Fran & Ollie, Luis Valdez, Joanna Verhaar, and my mother Emma Wallis for their kindness and educational and financial support.

And I once again thank the 250,000 children and adults in my audiences who graciously watched and participated in one or more of the 9000 performances I was able to perform in my all too short 30 year career as a puppeteer on the Central Coast of California (1983-2013); and I also thank the dozens of people who taught me how to carve and dress the puppets and the hundreds of people who hired and promoted our shows; and, as always, I thank you the reader.

Oh, remember that you are still alive and valuable; and it is imperative that you act like it—and that the child inside you and the children beside you thrive as artists and intelligent human beings wherever you are and wherever you go on and off our planet—and applaud yourself and each other: Yea!

CONTENTS:

FOR THE GOD OF SMALL CHILDREN:
THE HEART AND HANDS OF A PUPPETEER

A Memoir
By
Don Wallis

And they brought to him young children, that he might touch them. And the disciples rebuked them that brought them. Whom when Jesus saw, he was much displeased and says to them: Suffer the little children to come unto me and forbid them not: for of such is the kingdom of God. Amen I say to you, whosoever shall not receive the kingdom of God as a little child shall not enter into it. And embracing them and laying his hands upon them, he blessed them.

The Gospel of St. Mark, 10:13-16

In reality, the greatest of blessings come to us through madness, when it is sent as a gift of the gods.

Plato, quoting Socrates, in the *Phaedrus*

The world breaks everyone and afterward many are strong at the broken places. But those that will not break it kills. It kills the very good and the very gentle and the very brave impartially. If you are none of these you can be sure that it will kill you too but there will be no special hurry.

Ernest Hemingway, *A Farewell To Arms*

2

PART ONE

My booth stood on a lawn at the Santa Barbara County Fairgrounds and the international audience leaning against the front of it looked like a large canvas of beautiful shapes and colors on an easel. I peeked out from around the booth and said, "Ladies and Gentlemen, we now present the thousand year old English classic: The Mama, The Papa and The Silly Englishman Daddy Accidentally Threw The Baby Out the Window."

The audience responded with trepidation and laughter.

Judy leaned out over the proscenium arch at the very top of the booth. She had a large nose and a big smile that showed her teeth. She also had a yellow dress with red buttons and a small red hat.

"I wonder where that husband of mine is," she said. She had a deep voice. "I'm sure he's sleeping around the house here someplace. Me find him." And off she went.

Punch immediately snored himself out the side of the booth and back once and then twice out and back the other side.

"Ah, ha! Me hear him," Judy said.

Punch leaped up above the playboard. He showed his teeth too but he had a much larger nose and a much bigger smile than Judy. He wore a yellow shirt and pants with blue buttons and a large blue bicorne hat.

"There he is," Judy shouted. "Everybody yell, 'Punch!'"

"Punch!" the audience yelled.

Waking up, Punch lunged toward Judy shouting in his high-pitched voice, "What'd you wake me up for, Woman?"

"Punch, I gotta tell you something important," Judy shouted, blowing him back across the stage with her strong deep voice.

When he landed he said, "Important, is it?" Then he lightened his tone and asked, "What is it, Judy, my Luv?"

"I'm going downtown to get flowers for the dining room table."

"You woke me up to tell me you're getting flowers?" he shouted. Then he did a double take between her and the audience. "Downtown?"

"Yes," she said.

"Oh, Sweetheart. My little Goochie Goo."

"Ladies, I think he wants something," she said to the women in the audience.

"Oh, my Ravioli," Punch said. "My Goo Goo, Goo Goo, Ga Ga."

"Now, I know he wants something. What is it, Punch?"

"Judy," he asked, "would you get me a hamburger on a bun?"

Punch leaned way back over the playboard with his arms outstretched wide.

"One hamburger on a bun for Mr. Punch," she said.

"Yeah, Judy. A big one," he shouted.

"Okay."

"Everyone, clap your hands for my wonderful wifey. She's going to get me a hamburger."

Punch and the audience applauded loudly.

"Ah," Judy said. She fidgeted with her hands. "Just give me a little kiss on the cheek and I'll be running along."

Punch shook his head and ran to his end of the stage.

"Kiss me good-bye."

"No," Punch said and ducked his head down over the front of the playboard and spit. "Yuck."

"Punch."

Punch raised his head and asked the audience, "I have to kiss my wife good-bye?"

"Yes, you do, Sir," one of the Hindu girls shouted. Her mother stopped smiling but only for a second.

4

"I'm getting you the burger, Punch."

"All right," Punch said to the Hindu girl in the audience. "But you better not laugh at me, Shorty."

Both the mother and the young girl laughed.

"Punch, get over here."

Punch groaned as he walked over to Judy and smooched her loudly on the cheek. "Oh, my mouth." He spit. "Grown-up germs!"

Judy said to the audience, "Sometimes I think I'm married to a real silly man."

"You are!" the young Hindu girl shouted.

A smiling thin young boy laughed, bending his whole upper body.

Punch grabbed Judy in his arms and lifted her up and down. "Good-bye, Judy." He threw her down under the playboard. "Get me a hamburger!" And to the audience he said, "Guys, this ought to be great. I've got the whole house to myself for a couple of minutes. So, I'm gonna lie down and take a nap so I can stay up late tonight and watch the soccer on the Telly." He crashed on the playboard and snored immediately.

Returning quickly, Judy said, "I forgot to tell my husband to keep an eye on the baby."

"Punch!" she screamed.

Waking, he said, "What is it, Judy?"

"Be sure to keep an eye on the baby."

"What baby?"

"Our baby!"

"Oh, that baby." He turned to the audience and asked them, "I have to watch the baby?"

"Yes!" all the kids and most the adults shouted.

"Your wife said so," the smiling thin boy's little sister said. She said it so authoritatively, I wanted to laugh but I stopped myself, just barely.

"I'm getting you the burger, Punch."

"Okay."

Punch grabbed her in his arms. He bounced her up and down and threw her down beneath the playboard. "Get me the hamburger!" Then he told the audience, "You kids watch the baby."

"You have to!" one of the Euro-American kids screamed, shaking, outraged at Punch's behavior. "It's your baby!"

Punch lied back down and snored.

Then the baby cried, "Wa-a-a-h!"

Punch woke up and yelled, "Hey, who woke me up?"

"The baby!" the young Euro-American kid shouted.

"Whose baby?" Punch asked, searching the audience.

"Your baby!" the Euro-American kid screamed.

"My little kid woke his Papa up from a nap?"

"Yes," the same kid screamed.

"Where is it?"

The baby cried again.

Punch dropped down below the playboard and pulled up the crying baby. "Ladies, it's crying. What do you do with a crying baby?"

"Rock it," the smiling thin boy said.

"Rock it?" Punch raised his baby and bounced its bottom on the bed. "Rock."

"No," the boy said and laughed.

"Well, I've never done it before," Punch admitted.

Some kids in the front raised their forearms and moved them side-to-side.

"Oh," Punch said. He raised the baby and bounced its bottom twice on the bed. "Rock, rock. Is that it?"

"No!" the audience shouted.

"Like this," the excited Euro-American boy demonstrated swinging his forearms back and forth. "Gently."

"Ah, me can be gentle." Punch raised the baby and bounced its bottom three times on the bed. "Rock, rock, rock." He let go accidentally and threw the baby up into the air. It came down, bounced off the bed and fell on the floor. "Oh, oh. I think I made a little booboo." Punch looked unsuccessfully for the baby on the right side of the stage and then on the left. And then he looked down over the center of the stage beside the bed. "It must have fallen out the window. Me gonna get in T-R-O-U-B-L-E."

"Punch," Judy said from the top of the proscenium arch high above the rear of the stage. "I'm home with your hamburger."

"It's Judy. I'm going to lie down and pretend I'm asleep."

He lied down and started snoring.

Judy entered with a huge rubber toy hamburger. "Punch? That's strange. Usually my husband wakes right up when I bring food into the room."

Judy patted Punch hard with the hamburger. "Punch." Then she patted him again.

Eventually, Punch jumped up and grabbed the rubber hamburger away from her.

"Oh, Judy, you're home. You're so round," he said, talking to the rubber hamburger. "You smell so good. Hmmm. Kisses, Luv." He kissed it several times.

Judy faced the audience and said, "Sometimes I think I'm married to the silliest man. Is my baby here in the bed? I don't see it. Where's my baby?"

"Punch threw your baby out the window," one older kid said.

"Oh," she responded. "It's over here by the window."

"No," the same kid shouted. "It's O-U-T the window."

I stepped out from behind the booth and said, "Someone tell this woman exactly what happened to her baby and who did it."

"Punch threw your baby out the window," the excited Euro-American boy shouted, shaking and forcing the red into his cheeks.

Most the kids laughed. Some giggled.

"Don't worry," Judy said. "It happens all the time. My baby ate so much cake, cookies and ice-cream it got a bad tummy ache and it threw up out the window."

"No!" some kids screamed, nearly losing it. "Punch, your husband, threw it out the window!"

"Out the window?"

The red-cheeked kid shouted, "We've been trying to tell you."

"It's time for Mama to get the big pillow," Judy said.

"Couldn't you get the little pillow?" Punch asked. "The one you use for the Chihuahua on the sofa."

"You're going to get it," Judy said.

"I don't want it," Punch said, dropping the hamburger.

7

Judy exited and returned with a large pillow that matched the bedding on the bed.

Punch ducked.

"Are you people sure?" Judy asked the audience.

"We saw him."

"Are you positive?"

"Yes!"

"Good," Judy said. "Because it's not nice to be negative." She turned. "All the shenanigans you pulled this year, Mr. Punch. This one tops the cake."

Punch raised his head fast and asked, "Are we having cake?"

"Oh," Judy said, swinging the pillow around over her head.

Punch ducked again.

The baby cried.

"Oh, my baby," Judy yelled.

"Don't worry, Judy. Me get you the baby." Punch dived below the playboard.

Judy beamed. "Everybody, clap your hands for my wonderful husband."

"He's not wonderful," the excited young Euro-American boy shouted.

"He's going to get me my baby."

"No, he's not. He killed it!" the boy screamed.

Punch rose with the baby in his arms.

"Here it is, Judy. Him was asleep under the bed the whole time."

Leaning around the booth, I asked the audience, "Would some very kind person say: Judy, you have a beautiful baby."

"Judy, you have a beautiful baby," one Chicana mother said. She smiled broadly. Her husband chuckled, eyeing her and seeming truly amused that his wife was playing and able to tell a fib out of kindness.

Judy immediately asked the woman,"Do you really think so?"

Don't answer that, I thought.

"Yeah," Punch said, "him looks handsome like his Papa."

"You're not handsome," the Euro-American boy said. "You're an idiot!"

"Kiss the baby, Punch." Judy said.

"Do I have to kiss the baby?"

"Yes!" people shouted.

Someone said, "Kiss it."

Punch reluctantly walked over to the baby in Judy's arms. Looking at the baby, he said, "No, it's wrinkled and bald." Judy raised the baby to Punch's lips, quickly.

"Kiss it!"

Punch smooched the baby and immediately spit. "Oh, my lips. Yuck. Baby germs."

"Sometimes I just know I'm married to the silliest man in the whole world."

Punch raised his arms and addressed the audience.

"Everybody, clap your hands," he said, "for my wonderful family." The whole audience clapped their hands. "Louder," Punch commanded. "Me love them."

"They've been very nice to us, Punch."

"Yeah, right."

"Don't be silly."

"That's my middle name."

"I know."

Then Punch, Judy and the baby dropped below the playboard before the audience stopped applauding.

I stepped out from behind the booth quickly and faced the audience.

"Clap your hands louder, Folks, so you know you're alive. Louder, so you feel it. That's it." I encouraged them by clapping my own hands louder and faster every few seconds with a big old grin all over my face.

I looked at my beautiful little audience.

"Have a nice life, Everybody."

Oh, my God, I thought, watching the African-American sergeant lift his little girl up in his arms and then reach for his smiling thin little son's fingers with his free hand. The Hindu lady with the white teeth and smile also wrapped her two small children in her arms and turned them to walk away with their dad.

"Aren't you glad our lives aren't like that!" I said.

Before I took down my booth, I walked to a straw bale in the Petting Zoo and grabbed a piece and stuck it in my mouth.

~~~

Waking up and opening my eyes I look ahead at the mist in the car's high beams. I'm a little boy. I wait to see if another seventeen mule deer will leap off the mountain across the old one lane road and down the cliff. But tonight there are only five deer. And they descend the night sky with their legs spread like Bolshoi ballet dancers and their hooves strike the awesome light shining back into my eyes....

Milo and I trek down the steep bank to go fishing for trout in the creek behind the ranch house in the mountains between Templeton and Cayucos because Grandma Tillman said she would fry us what we caught for breakfast.

"Heads and tails, too?" Milo asked.

"Heads and tails, too," she said.

The creek is shallow and cold. We bait our hooks with red fish eggs; and during the next fifteen minutes we catch four 6-inch trout.

We figure Grandma will gut and scale them before she cooks them. But Milo's not sure and I'm not either.

Coming back up the bank, we hear the three dogs barking and jumping into the pickup with Grandpa and Dad out front.

Grandpa Tillman doesn't look like Walt Disney's Geppetto in *Pinocchio*, but he has the laugh. He smiles often and his smiles last for a long time.

Grandpa was too young to fight in WWI and then too old to fight in WWII. But he made his family stop speaking German at home the day President Franklin Delano Roosevelt declared war on Japan and Germany and they never spoke German again.

~~~

Two of Mom's brothers were drafted during the Korean War. Francis woke up alone on a hillside surrounded by hundreds of dead U.S. 6th Cavalry soldiers who didn't make it when the Chinese Army advanced during the night. Francis had emotional problems even before that morning in Korea and his younger brother Leonard had fallen off a horse and hit his head. Leonard later stood up on the firing range under machine gun fire in Boot camp and spent the rest of his life taking experimental drugs at VA hospitals in California. I first met Leonard when my parents visited him in Palo Alto in the 1950s.

~~~

When I was eleven in Manteca we got a television set and I got to watch Kukla, Fran & Ollie with the puppeteer Burr Tillstrom who I never saw because he was behind the booth holding the puppets up because they were little.

~~~

I cried when I had to leave my 5th grade teacher and the four other kids in my class at Rustic School. I had gone to school there off and on throughout my childhood, longer there than anywhere else. I tried to look back at my teacher and fellow students just once more when I got up out of my desk to follow my dad out of the room, but I couldn't see any of them because I was blind from the heavily salted tears in my eyes. My silent scream came after I got into the back bed of Dad's pickup beside Milo. I curled up in the fetal position and my body quaked horribly as I felt the ignition start and the accelerator descend as we started up Durham Ferry road from the only school, classmates and home I had ever really known.

~~~

Ten miles away that summer, Milo and I rode our bicycles together on dirt roads through the olive groves, strawberry fields and vineyards.

~~~

In sixth grade, I took long walks alone out into the nearest vineyard and up and down the road sometimes wondering what I wanted to do when I grew up. I also read a bunch of "The Most Unforgettable Character I Have Ever Met" stories in the *Reader's Digest* and liked them a lot. The stories were about common people who had unusual experiences like being lost in a blizzard or having to pull some hurt person out of a burning car. They faced their difficulties bravely out of a sense of responsibility, necessity or just plain old human decency and were successful.

That's when the old Merchant Marine showed up at the neighbor's place and moved into the second of the two barns next door. He wasn't an albino, just almost. He was short, skinny, bald and toothless. He had to be in his seventies. His P-coat could have held two of him. Springs he went back up north to Portland and Seattle. Falls he came south to Northern California. He walked, hitched and hopped freights. He had wintered in our neighbor's empty barn, he said, for the last three years. He could still hear and see well. He spoke softly but clearly. He told Milo and I stories while he heated his one can of Campbell's soup and his cup of coffee and ate his crackers and a can of corn beef, tuna or sardines and pulled out his papers and tobacco sack and rolled himself a cigarette.

He gave us a chocolate Hershey bar with almonds once, to split, and we got Mom to make him some chopped egg sandwiches a couple times and gave them to him.

I told him I had read the Illustrated Classics: *Treasure Island* and the one called *Moby Dick*.

He told us about the time he put an ice pick through the artificial septum of his nose and shook his head like a crazy man in front of the headhunters he and his mates accidentally came upon in the jungles on an island somewhere in the far South Pacific, and the headhunters, who all had bones through their noses, just stared at him and he and his friends got away.

He also said he saw a lot of fires on ships. During the two world wars, he feared the shells, mines and torpedoes. He said the engines were loud, the ships were cold and wet or hot and dry, the work was hard and the men were tough. He saw men fight, a man as big as my dad knifed in the belly and bleed to death and others swept overboard during monstrous storms and some of them drowned in the sea.

~~~

In the spring, I went on a field trip to Fishermen's Wharf in San Francisco. We also saw the Science Building and the Art Museum in Golden Gate Park.

I'm leaning against the pole railing of the white tour boat with blue trim. The fog on the Bay is cold and moist. It covers the water and bumps me in the face. I smell the salt and the seaweed of the ocean. Even the ocean's smell is deep. I think if I fell overboard I would get all wet and soggy. I'd probably drown. Maybe someone else would pull me out and I'd be saved and they would get all the credit for saving a dummy and I would be the dummy. Better to stay dry than to fall in this water. And it must be better to breathe even like a prisoner on Alcatraz than not to breathe at all.

I feel a tickling in my throat. I think I have been thinking so much so fast I have gotten a fever and I am catching a sore throat.

I think something must have happened because I am upset. I cannot imagine what the prisoners' lives are like. They must be bored like us kids now are at school. I am sure the prisoners get lunch but I am not so sure they get P.E. or recess.

I wonder if the old Merchant Marine went back up to Seattle. It is still hard for me to imagine how anyone can go off and live alone like that.

~~~

We left Manteca in the San Joaquin Valley and moved back to San Luis Obispo in 1958. Milo entered the 5th grade at Mission Grammar School and I the 7th, and we stayed enrolled there through High School.

~~~

My parents separated the summer between my freshman and sophomore years in High School. I was thirteen.

~~~

The twelve years 1958-1970, became the era of Sputnik and other satellites circling the earth and manned space flights to the moon. Children still had to practice ducking underneath their desks at school because we were being taught that the grownups in Russia and in our own country were probably going to wage a nuclear war and destroy the world. We also learned that it would probably be better for us to die instantaneously than to survive with radiation burns and disease. Everyone was sick with worry and counseling was not available for very many people. The 1950s' science fiction would become something a lot closer to reality and the myth of my family being inseparable would deconstruct and diffuse into so much additional atmospheric dust. There was so much going on around us, I think Milo and I got lost in whatever part of it we were watching at the moment.

I wondered a lot.

~~~

We lived through the Bay of Pigs and the three minutes to nuclear war between Kennedy's United States of America and Khrushchev's Union of Soviet Socialist Republics.

~~~

I wrestled with finding out whether or not I was a pacifist all through my senior year in High School and that summer and fall (1963-64). The gospels of Jesus of Nazareth, the tradition of St. Francis of Assisi, Leo Tolstoy's *The Kingdom Of God Is Within You*, Albert Schweitzer's *A Reverence For Life*, *The Autobiography of Mahatma Gandhi* and the life and work of Martin Luther King, Jr. led me to believe that it would be better for me to die than for me to harm anyone.

I applied for a full conscientious objector status in October.

~~~

My Draft Board sent me some information, a form and a notice that I would have to write "A Letter of Sincerity" to prove to them that I was sincere. They gave me a few weeks to write it and to fill out the form and mail it back to them and I did. Two weeks later, I got a notice granting me a full C.O. status for religious reasons.

I finally relaxed.

They could now draft me up to the age of forty years old to find an acceptable job and work for two years performing an alternative service outside my county so they could show people I was willing to bear a reasonable hardship for my country. But maybe they wouldn't draft me.

~~~

Late in 1967, I got my orders to look for work and a list of approved hospitals and Goodwill stores in the greater Los Angeles area. But I ran up to San Francisco.

I had studied acting at Cuesta College in San Luis Obispo for two years so I thought of working at a social center in the Mission District in San Francisco. I could help poor Chicano kids learn to read and write or start their own theater, but the center could only offer me a bed to sleep in and I would have to get a second job to make a living. Since I wanted time to write, I looked for something else.

I found a job at Alta Bates Community Hospital in Berkeley. I took it and calmed down again in the beginning for the first three or four months. I had a lot of new stuff to think about.

I started to feel guilty. Poor kids were being sent to kill or be killed in South Vietnam; and even younger kids were enlisting in the Viet Cong and the North Vietnamese Army to push us Americans out of their country. The bombs were dropping, the rockets firing, the babies crying, the combatants and noncombatants falling, screaming. People were getting hurt and dying, and I wasn't doing anything to stop it.

And silo per silo, the two greatest national powers still aimed their nuclear missiles at each other: the electronic guidance systems of the one (U.S.) versus the megatons and thrust of the other (U.S.S.R.). Both countries were powerful enough to destroy the human race and possibly the planet.

Working in the Nursery off the Maternity floor in the hospital, I more than once pictured all the wobbly and bouncy mothers, heavy as lead weights, walking on their swollen feet in all the maternity wards in Atlantic City and Kiev, New York and Leningrad, Washington D.C. and Moscow and all the hospitals and clinics all over the world.

~~~

Inge, the Nursery's head nurse, had grown up in Denmark during the Second World War. After the war, she studied nursing and came to New York City and got her U.S. nursing license. She moved to San Francisco and the East-Bay where she eventually ran the Nursery at Alta Bates Community Hospital, taught classes in the Lamaze method of childbirth and got her American citizenship. She was attractive, pleasant and a good speaker.

"I was a child," she said. "Even with German soldiers there, it wasn't always frightening. For the most part the Danish people did not collaborate with the Nazis and I'm proud of that. The threat of violence, the possibility of it, can be intimidating. It can be very important to not overreact."

That's all she said about it.

~~~

One day several months after I started working in the Nursery, Inge turned around, stepped back beside me and faced all the glassed rooms of her realm. She motioned with her hand. "See all these babies?" she said. "Our Raw, Fresh, and Gerber babies. When they leave here, their parents will take them to working class, middle class and upper class homes. Their parents will be blue-collar workers, university professors and business people. Each family will have their own cultural, educational and personality differences. These children will be raised differently. They will never again in their whole lives be treated as equally as they were here. We give each of them the same attention and identical care. That's our policy, and my nurses do it."

I nodded.

"That makes this Nursery a very special place then, doesn't it," I said.

~~~

Joshua weighed 2½ lbs. He had a large head and a small torso. He had to move his whole body to breathe. I'd stop and watch his chest expand and contract several times before I went back to taking the garbage out and to relining the wastebaskets with clean garbage bags.

I checked on Joshua even more on the weekends. I looked at his miniature arms, legs, hands, feet, fingers, toes, nose, mouth, eyes and ears. An orphan, he lay permanently on his back in his rectangular plastic isolette case with the two thinly-covered armholes on both of the two longer sides for the nurses and doctors to reach him when necessary to wash and change him or more importantly to touch him when his heart and lungs quit and the alarm on the top of his isolette went off and all the Nursery staff would stand and look immediately toward his isolette to triangulate their location to see who was closer and the closest would run to his isolette, shove their hand through an armhole and touch him tenderly with the tip of a finger to restart his heart, lungs and brain to bring him back to life.

It caused Joshua brain damage whenever he stopped breathing and none of us knew how much, especially on the worst days back in the beginning when he would stop breathing up to eight or nine times a day.

I remember watching Joshua and thinking he looked like a large frog wiggling to free himself pinned down like frogs my dad had gigged with the three barbs at the end of an eight-foot pole in the canal on our small Manteca farm. I remember the meals of frog legs Mom had fried and served us late at night… and I'd feel bad sometimes for thinking Joshua was food for some nonhuman thing in Nature instead of being an orphaned premature baby some fortunate human parents would one day hold, feed and love.

"That a boy, Joshua," I told him. "That a boy."

His body flexed and relaxed, and flexed.

~~~

Come on, Joshua, I thought. Live.

~~~

January 1969, I stood in Sproul Plaza with ten-thousand Berkeley students protesting the U.S. war in Vietnam and police violence on campus. After the student leader's speech a member of the administration came out of Sproul Hall and told us to leave. But the campus newspaper, the faculty committee and the Student Council had all endorsed the protest and the student strike so we stayed.

Thirteen riot cops sprinted out across the front of Sproul Hall. Their white helmets and black leather jackets gleamed; their gray visors shaded their faces and enlarged the exaggerated sockets of their eyes. They stood like a row of dark statues in a wax museum: each one threatening to come alive.

The crowd became silent.

Something like a cool breeze moved through me and down between the legs of the person behind me and hid in the shadows about a hundred feet back.

The Captain pushed up his visor and barked his orders to his men.

I stay here, I thought. Sit down, or lie down: whatever it takes. No matter what happens—anything—I don't leave.

The Captain and his men took two steps forward and kept on coming. Their brown riot clubs bounced and banged against their belts.

"We're not leaving!" a student shouted, throwing a brown bag over the riot cops' heads. "You bastards leave us alone!"

Twelve more riot cops came up out of the basement. Another twelve came out from around the right side of the building. Both groups ran toward the steps and down them.

I backed up—straight back—ten or twelve feet.

The Captain and thirty-six of his riot cops stood in a long line across the foot of the steps.

"You Pigs, get out of here!" one of the student leaders up near the front yelled.

The Captain glared.

The student threatened the Captain with his fist. "Go kill somebody somewhere else!" he shouted.

"That one, there!" the Captain said, extending his left arm parallel to the ground. "That one right there!"

The two cops beside the Captain lunged toward the student, grabbed his arms and shoved him to the ground. His knees hit the pavement. Saliva flew out of his mouth. The muscles in his face bulged and stretched when he threw his head and hair back between the clubs bouncing off the riot cops' hips. He screamed. His whole body shook. Then he screamed again. He dropped his head to his chest and reached for his stomach with the flexed palms and fingers of his hands. The two cops picked him up by his armpits and started dragging him off between the cops in front of the steps.

"No more!" one student shouted.

"Not one more of us!" another student screamed.

The two cops mounted the steps panting, jerked the student leader toward them hard and kept on going.

The student's limp body dangled from their arms. The dark soles of his shoes rose slowly up the steps.

The Captain shouted over his shoulder and pulled down the plastic visor on his helmet.

I stared at his gloves and at the handle of the gun in the black holster on his hip.

Students near me threw lunch sacks and paper cups.

Half the cops hunched their backs and crouched low to the pavement. Two cops near the Captain rammed the backs of their helmets against the black fur collars on their jackets and ducked when an open milk carton leaving a trail of milk behind it soared past them toward the building.

Four guys ran toward the cops. First one took a swing at the Captain and backed up fast on his heels when the Captain swung his fist over the guy's head. Second one leaped into the air behind two cops who turned to help the Captain. He landed on the backs of their shoulders and grabbed them by their necks. Third one rammed his fist up under another cop's visor, spun around fast and sprinted back toward the crowd. Fourth one slid legs-first between two cops, turned his shoulders and slammed his hands down flat on the pavement.

The two cops dragging the student leader pulled him hard down into the basement. He was gone.

Who'll stop them from doing anything they want to him? I wondered. Don't make them angrier, I thought. Not down there all by yourself.

Six guys in light blue overalls ran out of the basement in pairs. Each pair carried a metal rack containing black canisters.

"Blue Meanies!" someone in the crowd shouted.

"Tear gas," someone shouted.

The first pair of guys in overalls reached the bottom of the steps and sat their rack down, pulled out a couple of canisters and hurled them.

"Look out!" someone screamed.

Students backed up to get away from the gas-leaking canisters rolling around between their legs. A big guy with broad shoulders started coughing harshly when the gas in front of him started swirling upward around his head. The redhead beside him panicked. She held her hands over her eyes while the outer layers of the gas seeped deeper and deeper into her nose and mouth.

A thin blond guy entered one of the gas clouds, grabbed the canister and hurled it at the cops.

One of the riot cops swat at it with his club.

Seeing him miss it, the cop beside him picked it up off the pavement and threw it back into the front of the crowd.

Gas moved toward me over the pavement. I pulled my arms in to keep from bumping into the people beside me. When I sensed the gas entering my head and lungs, I closed my mouth and tried to stop breathing through my nose.

The Captain and his thirty-six cops grabbed their clubs and ran toward the front of the crowd.

All my weight went back on my heels.

"Here they come!" someone near me shouted.

People pushed. I turned and started to run. I stumbled forward twenty yards.

"Keep moving!" someone behind me screamed.

I raised the palm of my hand toward the top of my face and smeared the sweat flooding my forehead with my wrist. I saw the small water fountain three feet ahead of me. Its short concrete wall rose toward my knees. Stop, I thought, or you'll hit it.

Stop moving.

I opened my mouth. I grabbed the top of the wall of the fountain. Something tasted green in my stomach. I was afraid I was going to vomit. I blinked tears out of the burning corners of my eyes.

Someone rammed an elbow into the small of my back.

Stop pushing.

Everyone near the fountain in front of the Student Union coughed uncontrollably. Some choked. I swerved around the fountain, holding one of my arms over my stomach.

Into the Student Union, I thought. Inside.

~~~

Within a few months people turned a dirt parking lot near Telegraph Avenue into an urban park. They built swings, put up a slide and planted flower and vegetable gardens. Trespassing… on state property.

There used to be a dorm on it, I think, but the University tore the building down and just left the bare lot. Chancellor Heyns threatened to fence it off.

Two-hundred-and-fifty Highway patrolmen invaded People's Park. They showed up with a surveillance helicopter at 5 a.m. Governor Reagan had the chancellor put up a metal fence around the whole thing to keep everyone out. Six-thousand students and hippies marched down Telegraph toward the Park. Kids broke windows out of the Bank of America on the corner at Telegraph and Durant and threw rocks and tear gas canisters back at the police.

~~~

I got on the College Avenue bus. I sat next to a heavyset African-American woman with a big red purse and a bigger white and royal blue shopping bag.

"Is that tear gas?" someone on the bus asked.

"Why aren't you stopping, Driver?" someone else shouted.

"We're supposed to stop. There're policemen all over the corner you just passed."

"Calm down, Folks," the driver said. "No one back there was stopping traffic. I'm going to turn left up here."

"Well, a policeman's banging on the bus back here. Can't you hear it?"

The driver continued driving up College.

"Oh, my god," someone said. "It is tear gas. It's another riot."

"Calm down, everybody," the driver said. "I'll turn left here and we'll go around it."

"That cop's still banging on the bus back here," the guy in the back said. "He wants us to stop."

"All right, now," the driver said and started to turn left. "We're gonna go around it, Ladies and Gentlemen. Just like I've been doing."

He turned and I saw the link chain fence around People's Park.

People on the left side of the bus stood up. Some stepped into the aisle. One leaned against my shoulder and the back of my seat to look out the right side of the bus.

"Maybe you're doing the right thing," the guy in the back said. "That cop stopped pounding. He stopped running, too."

"Okay," the driver said. "Everybody, quiet. I'll get us out of here."

The bus entered the outer edge of a huge tear gas cloud.

~~~

I looked at the gas.

"Hear it?" someone shouted.

"Sit down, People," the driver said. "Sit down."

"Look," someone said. "They're shooting."

"Shooting?" a thin elderly woman asked.

"They use birdshot for riots," the driver said. "The police aren't going to hurt these people."

"Right," a young black man behind me said sarcastically. Then he laughed. "Birdshot? They don't use birdshot on the Brothers." He hardened his voice. "Not on the Panthers, they don't."

"They're going to kill somebody," someone said. "Look!"

"They're not killing anybody," the driver said. "I'm driving you out of this. Now, everybody, sit down."

The bus moved slowly. Then it stopped.

Alameda sheriff's deputies and Highway patrolmen attacked students and hippies, and the students and hippies made random attempts at fighting back. Isolated individuals threw rocks, garbage and trash while a few of the Alameda sheriff's deputies aimed and fired their shotguns at specific individuals and small groups of demonstrators. Buckshot. Blood.

People on the bus screamed. The ones outside yelled from being gassed or wounded.

"Dear Lord," said the heavyset African-American woman sitting beside me next to the window.

I heard her praying.

"Dear Jesus. Don't let anyone be hurt. Not today. No more babies, Lord. No more children. Not Black, or White. Please, help everyone on this bus, Lord, and every one of these poor troubled people outside and my son Jerome, Lord, overseas. Oh, my precious, precious Jesus. Jesus. No more young black soldiers, Lord. No more young white college kids. I know you, Lord. I ask you, Lord. Take me. If you have to, Lord. Take me, Jesus, instead."

The tear gas grew thicker and darker outside the window behind her head. Her white teeth looked bluish or even a greenish-gray so near her bright red lipstick.

"Lord, amen," she concluded.

The bus started moving again.

~~~

The next morning I heard the rumbling noise of the truck transmissions changing gears.

I heard the first two convoys pass before I saw the third. Drab-green military vehicles moved up University Avenue toward campus. I counted three trucks and two jeeps. The trucks carried armed National Guardsmen and the second jeep pulled a small trailer with a larger gun mounted on it.

Three young guardsmen stood holding rifles on the corner as I crossed the street where I waited to catch my bus to get to work. They wore helmets, khakis and laced-up high-top leather boots. They had short hair but one had a thin, dark mustache. They looked clean cut, and so serious and determined. They must have been pretty scared.

I was.

I saw three armed guardsmen on every intersection all the way up University, Shattuck, Telegraph and College. A small force: but only the start of a much larger invasion. Army trucks and jeeps were roaming the streets all over Berkeley.

People at Herrick Hospital (the General Hospital closer to People's Park) had told people at Alta Bates about the victims of the riot through the hospital grapevine. James Rector, a young African-American man from Oakland, had been killed and Alan Blanchard, a young Euro-American artist from Berkeley, had been blinded permanently. Seventy to a hundred-and-ten people had been wounded and many were still under hospital care.

At work I picked up trash, swept, mopped, dusted and cleaned some glass windows and a few more isolettes in the Nursery.

Sad, frightened and wondering what would happen next, I thought about the tanks the Russians had moved into Prague, Czechoslovakia, and the internment camps Americans had had for the Japanese-Americans during WWII. I thought about the Watts riot. I thought about WWIII. I thought about armed police and soldiers camping in the park. I thought about them overpowering the swings and flowers, hunching over them, like black ants conquering the leftovers of a picnic like black spots floating across my eyes.

~~~

The National Guardsmen, who had looked so young this morning now looked older, and tired of course. Their bodies sagged. They looked dispirited under the weight of their orders, heavy helmets, rifles and boots.

The guardsmen were Californians, at least, and some were even locals, and not a bunch of rural rednecks from Alabama and Mississippi or even from Florida and Texas like many of the Alameda sheriff's deputies were. As I got off the bus, I avoided eye contact with the two guardsmen on the corner. The third was now on the diagonal corner across the street. I crossed with the light very mindful of the boundaries of the crosswalk and then I turned to the right up the sidewalk to the front of my apartment building on California Street and I looked back over my shoulder to confirm that there really were no rifles aimed at my back.

Upstairs, I stuck my head out my kitchen window.

The mustached guardsman out on the corner saw me looking at him, raised his rifle and aimed it straight at my face. He pointed his loaded rifle at my head.

I believe I fumed for the next five minutes, staring down the outer contours and the interior darkness of his rifle barrel, before the young mustached guardsman finally shut his eyes for a flick of a second, relaxed his finger on the trigger and lowered his rifle. The first thing I thought of was all the tired musicians in the world lowering their instruments when they had finished playing the last piece of their last set. This guy was a weekend soldier. And that made him dangerous.

The guardsman smiled. His buddy jabbed him in the arm, and they both laughed.

~~~

In the morning I saw out the bus window hundreds of guardsmen holding bayonet-attached rifles lined up along several blocks of Shattuck and Telegraph.

It was illegal now for more than three people to congregate together in public. The guardsmen were detaining groups of four or more people who were out together. So I was amazed when I saw three young women with flowers striking up friendly conversations with soldiers and putting the stem-end of daisies down the soldiers' rifle barrels. I saw dozens of other longhaired, bright-eyed and friendly hippie girls and university coeds in groups of threes on Shattuck and Telegraph. The whole collective mass of tanned blonds, freckled redheads, pale brunettes and olive-skinned black haired girls were wearing cotton Nehru-collared blouses, snug bell-bottom jeans, long loose paisley skirts, raw-leather sandals and silver and gold earrings. They made giving and receiving flowers look so easy.

There was a curfew now but no one was clear when it started. Undeterred, a group of religious activists (Quakers, Methodists and Catholics, etc.) had a silent candlelight vigil that night and walked from People's Park to the wounded still recovering at Herrick Hospital.

~~~

The Guard trapped hundreds of students in an alley near the Student Union and a helicopter came in and sprayed them with a more powerful tear gas than usual. They also stopped a peaceful march on Shattuck at University. Thousands of marchers including Joan Baez and her mother were rounded up at bayonet point. The celebrities and four hundred other people were bused to Santa Rita Prison farm.

After all the arrests, someone got Governor Reagan to pull the Guard off the streets and hide them somewhere out of sight.

Three of the five Highway patrolmen still inside the fence at People's Park were hanging out by the slide. The other two were farther off over in the gardens. One of the three was climbing up the steps and one was sitting high up on the slide holding the short sides to keep from sliding down. Then he let go and slid down the slide, waving his arms over his helmet and giggling like he was having fun doing it. The one at the foot jumped out of the slider's way while the one on the steps hurried up to the top to take his turn.

The other two Highway patrolmen in the gardens picked up a shovel and a hoe. Using the hoe as a golf club, the one whacked at the stakes and demolished the string bean and tomato plants.

~~~

People tend to avoid social confrontation. Even in California most people won't stick their necks out in public or participate in a protest demonstration. But both the famous San Francisco poets and the

25

general population of Berkeley came out to express their outrage against the authorities' misuse of power. The Beat-era poets read their work to two-thousand people in an old professional theater in San Francisco. And the locals, nearly fifty-thousand strong, walked lively and peacefully down Shattuck Avenue through the Berkeley financial district on Memorial Day.

The poetry reading in San Francisco was at night so I went. I wanted to see Lawrence Ferlinghetti, Gary Snyder, Kenneth Rexroth, the Dominican Brother Antoninus, Michael McClure and Richard Brautigan and maybe more of the seventeen Northern California poets. The possibility of seeing and hearing them all on one evening in San Francisco for a political cause in Berkeley was very exciting. And I did see them. And it was, to me, a very exciting historical event.

Fifty-thousand people marched. They had such a large peaceful demonstration Governor Reagan lost his only excuse for martial law in Berkeley. It does not look good for the authorities to use force and violence against white nonviolent, law and order, tax-paying citizens in the U.S. So, Reagan had to get the troops out before a bigger problem occurred. The Guard had stayed seventeen days in Berkeley. Now the guardsmen could go home to their families and friends.

~~~

I looked through the glass wall on the side of the Nursery. Sunlight tingled through the blue sky as it did through my eyelashes.

"Where's Joshua, Inge?" I asked.

"He's been transferred," she said.

"Where?" I asked.

"He gained enough weight, so… another health agency in Oakland," Inge said. "We can't keep preemies. He'll be put up for adoption eventually. There are lots of couples who want babies."

I stood still, stopped talking and stared at my memory of how Joshua looked when he breathed.

In my twenty-two-year-old imagination, Joshua was lying on a bed of illuminated balloons. The hundreds of rainbow-colored balloons floated over the water to Hawaii, to British Columbia and to Baja. They floated over the land to Oaxaca, to the islands of the Caribbean.

They floated out of all the nurseries in all the hospitals and all the mangers in all the stables on earth, the moon and the planets in all the galaxies in the cosmos. The darkness became full of sunlight and space filled with air. All the babies in creation were blowing balloons like bubbles between their soft puff-bubbly little lips.

"Don't stop," I said.

~~~

I saw a tall young woman in her late 20s step out of the elevator this side of Maternity, turn and start to enter the Nursery. She stopped and stiffened just inside the open double doorway. Something was wrong. People don't gain the weight of marble or the hardness of bronze. Not the way she did, not that fast. Not as fast as the snap of a finger.

"Hope," I said to the older nurse beside me.

Hope and I were both staring at the young woman as she raised her head and spread her mouth and screamed.

"I want my baby! My baby! I want to hold my baby. Oh, God, let me hold my baby!" the tall young woman screamed, "somebody's baby! Please!"

Hope grabbed my forearm and squeezed real hard.

Inge stood up at the Nurses' Station, turned and ran to the tall young woman in the doorway. She wrapped her arms around the younger woman and held her tight.

"Oh, my," I whispered to myself, wrapped in a huge thick curtain of silence that dropped through the light swirling from the ceiling to the floor all along the walls, the windows and the double doorway of the smaller shrinking room.

"It's the woman who lost her baby," Hope said, and then loosened her grip on my arm. "A crib death."

"Here?" I asked.

"No. Some babies go home and are healthy for a few weeks or even months. No sign of a problem and then one morning their parents find them dead in their cribs. They just die during the night for some reason or another."

"No, Hope," I said.

"It's not the parents' fault," Hope said. "It's nothing they did, nothing they didn't do. But they blame themselves. This woman lost her daughter a few months ago. It's a horrible thing they have to live with for the rest..."

"Of their lives," I said.

"Of her life," I corrected myself.

Hope patted my shoulder with the palm of her small New England hand and then she went to change a baby.

I cleaned and watched.

Inge called Sharon, the younger nurse, to get a chair. She sat the woman down in the very center of the Nursery. Then she got Sharon to bring the woman a baby and let her hold it for about ten minutes. Then, because Inge was Inge and maybe brilliant, she got Sharon to bring the woman a second baby and let her hold both babies for over half an hour longer while she stood next to her, mothering.

Long before the tall young woman left, I turned my back toward her, stepped into the tall shadows in one of the corners of the Nursery and started crying. I couldn't hear anything but the mousy sounds of my own whimpering.

Why did I want to be here if I didn't want to feel any of the pain in this world? I asked myself. My eyesight dimmed graying everything. I saw how distinct and unreachable Inge, Hope and Sharon and the tall young woman and all the babies in the Nursery looked.

When the tall young woman finished holding the babies and got up to leave, Inge said, "You can come back here and hold a baby any time you want to, any time."

I stared at the young woman's back, feeling something in all of us was leaving forever while I watched her walk toward the elevator.

PART TWO

I went backstage and inserted my hands into Hansel and Gretel.

They entered the stage looking exhausted.

"I dropped breadcrumbs on the ground so we could find our way home," Hansel said. "From the road to where we got lost in the forest."

"But the birds ate all the breadcrumbs," Gretel said.

"Yeah. But I didn't think of that," Hansel said. "I'll find the road and save us."

Gretel looked off in the distance. She pointed. "Look. There's a house, Hansel, with a road in front."

"With peanut brittle, taffy and jelly donuts," Hansel yelled. "All over it." He ran toward the house and started licking it. "Yum, yum, yum."

Gretel ran to the far corner of the house and exited the stage. "There's cotton candy and jelly beans back here," she shouted.

Hansel took another big lick.

"Wow, I found the road and the cookies and candy," Hansel said. "I saved us."

"Who found it?" Gretel asked, off-stage.

"I did," Hansel said. "I was looking for it."

"No, you didn't," she said.

From inside the Gingerbread house came a scratchy old voice singing:

"Scrape the bristles off a pig.
Find an apple, or a fig.
Light the oven, cook the pork.
I like children, tall or short…"
Hansel froze in place.

"Gretel?" he whispered.

The old voice inside the house continued singing:
"Little pig, or tiny mouse.
Who is eating up my house?"
"Oh, oh," Hansel said, weakly.

An ugly old Witch entered the stage. She faced the audience and said, "Hello, you little geese."

"We're not geese," a chubby boy with a red candied apple in the front yelled.

"Then you're an ugly duckling," the Witch said and laughed.

"I'm a swan," an older man with a green wool cap shouted.

"And I'm prettier than Sleeping Beauty," the Witch said. She laughed, giggled and laughed again. "I am," she said. Then she turned and lowered her head and looked straight into Hansel's eyes. "Hello, Pudding," she said.

"I was hungry… and, and," Hansel said, trembling.

"Did you like the taffy and the donuts?" she asked.

"Yes, thank you," Hansel said. "And the peanut brittle was very tasty."

"I have hot macaroni and cheese and pizza inside."

"I haven't had pizza in months," Hansel said. "Our new mother never feeds me anything."

The Witch put her hand on Hansel's back and said, "Do you like chocolate?"

"I like chocolate better than anything," Hansel said.

"Good," the Witch said. "I've got a birdcage stuffed with a huge chocolate turkey."

"A chocolate turkey," Hansel said, giggling.

The Witch leaned over the playboard toward the chubby boy in front of the audience.

"Goose," she said.

The boy laughed and shook his head as he tried to take a bite out of his red candied apple.

The Witch turned toward Hansel and pushed him into the house. "Come inside," she said and screamed in delight as she exited the stage.

Backstage, I raised the backdrop to reveal a second backdrop showing the interior of the house. The audience now saw the front of the oven and a table with piles of nuts and berries on it.

"You'll be, oh, so delicious," the Witch laughed entering the stage. She immediately looked over the playboard and asked the chubby boy's sister, "Aren't I the most beautiful Lady you've ever seen?"

"You're mean, and ugly, you skinny hag," the heavyset girl shouted, excitedly.

The girl's mother turned toward her and patted her on her head.

"That was very cruel," the Witch said, almost crying. "I may be the most beautiful woman here, but... but... That hurt my feelings."

"Good!" the girl screamed.

Gretel entered the stage, demanding, "Where's my brother?"

The Witch froze.

"She goosed him and put him in a birdcage," one of the older boys in the far back of the audience shouted.

I paused. A lot of people, including me, broke out laughing.

"Your brother's eating a cupcake in the birdcage while I fix him a healthy chicken breast sandwich with a cup of rice and mushroom soup and a small garden salad with raspberry vinaigrette dressing. If you want to help, you can check on the oven. Just stick your head in to make sure it's hot enough to bake Pudding," the Witch said. "And the bread for his sandwich."

"Okay," Gretel said enthusiastically. But then she stopped.

"I don't know how. My stepmother never teaches me how to do anything." Gretel started to cry. "Oh, please show me how to stick my head into the oven so we can bake bread for my little brother's sandwich. Please, hurry. He's starving."

"Oh, Girlie," the Witch said, "just open the oven door and put your head in all the way, like this." The Witch stuck her head all the way into the oven. "See?" the Witch said.

"Yes," Gretel said. "I see."

Gretel pushed the Witch into the oven, closed the door and held it shut.

"Let me out of here," the Witch screamed. "It's hot. I'm burning. Help! I'm dying." She screamed in anguish several more times until she died.

Gretel exited the far side of the stage to get Hansel.

They reentered the stage together.

"How did you know she was a witch?" Hansel asked.

"Nice ladies don't serve little boys cupcakes in birdcages," Gretel said. "They have them sit properly at the table. And they don't get to eat their dessert until after they eat their lunch."

"Oh."

"Now grab some nuts and berries and we'll take them home to Daddy."

Hansel hesitated.

"What's wrong?" Gretel demanded.

"You're the one who saved us, Gretel, not me. And you found the road in front of the Gingerbread House, too. I didn't," Hansel said.

"We're both trying to save each other, right?" Gretel said.

"Right," Hansel agreed.

"Come on, little Brother," Gretel said.

"Okay," Hansel said. "I'll lead the way."

And he followed her out and they ran home down the road together.

The audience started clapping.

I went out front to get the audience to applaud themselves for helping my puppets. Then I passed the hat.

The older man in the green wool cap added five dollars to the dollar bills and quarters in my collection bucket. He shook my hand and with a German accent he told me he had first seen *Hansel & Gretel* after WWII when he was a hungry little boy in an orphanage in Munich. He worked internationally on oil rigs now, he said. Neither of us ever had a sister. I was glad to have had some wonderful cousins, I said.

"Good," I said.

I felt great. Then I went and ate a very large late dinner and I laughed again and again for no apparent reason.

~~~

Some illnesses come on slowly.

I felt a little light-headed.

I became a needy person.

I needed to know that the preemie Joshua I had known at Alta Bates Community Hospital in Berkeley was okay and that he'd grow up to be president and not have an emotional collapse like Presidents Abraham Lincoln and Lyndon Baines Johnson.

I needed my girlfriend Rena to stop walking so fast. It was nice of her to go with me when I went to see the psychiatrist at the Berkeley Herrick Hospital, but I couldn't stop wondering what she told him when she went in to talk to him.

The doctor assumed I had taken LSD and was having a bad trip. He said my friends should put me on a bus and send me to Napa State Hospital where at that time they had a special program for artistic young people.

Then we left and went to a drugstore. I was trying to figure out why Rena asked the pharmacist for the seven cents we were short, so we could buy the Thorazine the psychiatrist wanted me to start taking immediately. The druggist also gave me a glass of water so I could take a pill right there in the drugstore, which I did.

Outside, I wanted to lie down on the high ground in the street where the cars were passing because it looked like the safest place for me to take a nap. But Rena wouldn't let me lie down in the middle of the street. She walked me all the way home because I was so tired all of a sudden, sleepy and weak.

I needed to stop seeing dead children all over the lawns, lots and driveways and the mountains, fields and roads on the planet, but I didn't tell her because I was beginning to forget.

~~~

Ed Schum stood next to Jim and Roberta Owen. Roberta smiled when she saw I was waking up smiling glad to see them, but Jim didn't. He looked serious.

"Hi, Jim," I said, loudly in a high-pitched voice.

Ed said, "When I first got here we talked nonstop for almost an hour. I would have sworn there was nothing wrong with him. Then it was like his mind went and he stopped making sense."

"I'm tired," I said.

I imagined I was dead and wind was tossing my spirit around above the ocean.

"Really tired."

~~~

Jim and Roberta drove south to San Luis Obispo in their old Renault rattling down the highway at its top speed of 38 miles per hour. I slept in the backseat, pressing my fleshy-face against the glass window behind Jim, or staring at the moon, the planes and the clouds. I imagined the construction cranes I saw throughout the South Bay were giant dinosaur skeletons lurking overhead.

Jim made me a bed on the couch near his wooden desk and small bookcase.

I slept, protected.

"Maybe you should sign yourself into the Mental Health Clinic," Jim said. "Just for three days, Don. Then you can sign yourself out whenever you want."

"Locked up?" I asked.

"It's a clinic."

~~~

I saw a small headline in Jim's L.A. Times. It said a twelve year-old girl named Yvonne had died from a three-story fall inside the warden's house on Alcatraz. The girl's father was Richard Oakes, a Mohawk from New York, who was the spokesman for the occupiers. Many Indian protesters had brought their children to live on the island.

I pictured some little kids wearing their warm sweaters and jackets playing on the walkways and ledges, and then Yvonne now motionless. Dead.

"Don?"

"Jim?"

"Yes, Don?"

"I think I'm really sick."

Jim took me in the morning. I signed myself into the San Luis Obispo Mental Health Clinic.

A woman with shoulder length black hair took me into a small narrow room and had me sit across from her at a table. She showed me inkblot pictures and asked me questions. Another woman gave me a larger dose of Thorazine and walked me down a hallway into a large room. I passed some sick people. The woman unlocked a door with a tiny rectangular window and walked me to an empty single bed with a white sheet and a gray knit bedspread for a blanket which was all right because I had to lie down pretty quick before the dark came all the way into my head and spread back out through the whole room. The woman left, and I slept.

I lived on Thorazine there in the locked ward for a-million-and-a-half-years... over the next three days.

~~~

For the first half million years I kept waking up ever so slightly and backing away into sleep.

~~~

For the next half million years the stars kept looking real bright until the sun finally rose from way over there to all the way over here in the opposite direction.

~~~

For the last hundred-thousand years I held the paint bowl up toward the lit wall of a cave. I dipped the stick into the paint and continued drawing.

~~~

I held the stylus and inked the marks on the papyrus, sweating like a slave rolling a stone under the burning sun. I hobbled out of Egypt amongst a vast multitude of people to be unified as one among the One behind the One under the One to be released and reorganized to survive for a little while longer.

~~~

I heard the trumpets and the clash of swords and shields.

I felt a cut burn its sting across the length of my arm and my non-coagulated blood dropping into the open mouth of the ground.

~~~

I didn't want to run, so I didn't, when the enemy drove us into the bottom of the ditch and stabbed me in the belly with a muddied bayonet.

~~~

Because I needed some buddies I crawled forward to get to the wounded Yanks, Brits, French and Germans moaning, crying and screaming out in the open between the trenches. I tried to carry and drag them back to doctors and medicine because they were there and I was there. There were thousands of them waiting.

~~~

I ate my bread and drank my water with as much human dignity as I could, sitting on the edge of the cot in my pacifist's cell in New York City, while my countrymen launched the Normandy invasion and firebombed all the big cities in Japan. I imagined my flesh and bones melting in the heat along with the children in Hiroshima and Nagasaki. It was confusing because everyone seemed so intent on killing to stay alive.

~~~

I saw a monk kneel in the street out in the center of an intersection away from the hanging banners and the painted wood facades of the buildings. The monk raised a faded red can and poured gasoline on his yellow robe. Saturated, he lowered the can and reached for a metal flint lighter that he had gotten from a rural French priest in 1950. The priest had gotten it from a young American G.I. at the end of World War II before the priest came to Vietnam in the late 40s. The monk chose to use it now in the middle 1960s not to char his body but to offer some light on the U.S. foreign intervention inside his country and on the oppression of his people with his hands folded eventually in prayer and his breath expiring off the flaming tips of his fingers.

~~~

And the Czech university student, Torch Number One, burned like a human hunk of meat that had fallen off a grill and down into a campfire so the Russians might witness his commitment to resist their invading army occupying his native soil. Like the elderly Vietnamese monk had done for Americans. Like I would like to have done for

38

everyone, but I was afraid to do it for anyone. I felt selfish, and ashamed.

~~~

The Nurse gave me more pills and water in small paper cups. And once when she left, I walked up to the small window in the door and looked out. I saw people outside in the Open Ward. I reached down for the doorknob and I tried to turn it but I couldn't get it to move. I was locked in. And I wanted out of the Locked Ward and out of the Mental Health Clinic as fast as possible because I knew, even if I didn't know anything else, that I wasn't the one who was crazy.

~~~

If my Bavarian grandmother Theresa Tillman was overweight, then my Prussian psychologist was skinny. My happy-go-lucky grandmother managed her kitchen and everyone in it with a fun-loving spirit. The overly serious psychologist commanded paperwork and people, like she was declaring war on everything in a way that made everyone around her a resistant obstacle—or the enemy.

I liked my grandmother.

The psychologist sat behind a wooden table, facing me.

"You are a draft dodger, Mr. Wallis?"

Confused by her question before it hit me hard, I smiled.

"A protester?" she added.

I looked around for support: below her elbows, behind her dark shoulders and above her thick short gray hair.

"An artist?" she asked.

She looked buried alive in grays: her complexion, her hair and her clothing.

"A hippie?" she said.

Cold air spread over the hot surface of my skin while I turned toward the people sitting on my right. They all looked seriously concerned about something, and none of them looked me in the eyes. My therapist raised his fist to his mouth and coughed slightly through the opening between his first finger and his thumb.

Is something bad going to happen to me? I wondered.

"Can you speak, Mr. Wallis?" the psychologist asked.

"I went to high school here," I said.

"What, Mr. Wallis? You went to high school here?"

"Un, huh."

"Yes, we know that. Most of our boys are proud to fight for our country."

"Yes, Ma'am. I was born here. I…"

I wanted to ask her why she sounded so sad. She looked too thin to be healthy. She must have been hurting from something like other people in the Clinic. But my throat and mouth wouldn't move, and I didn't have the energy to speak.

I bobbed my head a few times and closed my eyes.

The psychologist kept talking, but now to the others in the room.

"Mr. Wallis is withdrawn, delusional and unable to care for himself appropriately. Clearly, it appears hallucinogens, illegal drugs, have intensified his condition. Drugs being so prevalent among these kinds of people, obviously."

I don't take drugs, I thought.

The Thorazine? I wondered.

An accident?

"It's my opinion this patient is a perfect candidate for the care facility at Camarillo State Mental Hospital."

AN INSANE ASYLUM?

"You agree, Dr. Middleton?"

Like my Uncle Leonard drugged and imprisoned for life at the veteran's hospital in Palo Alto, I thought.

"I do not," Dr. Middleton said.

What?

"You don't agree?" the psychologist asked.

"No," Dr. Middleton said. "I don't."

The psychologist glared at Dr. Middleton on my right.

The old medical doctor was obese. He sat out all over the edges of his solid wood chair: his body rolling out of his giant suit beneath his Tolstoyan hair and beard.

"There is no evidence of violence to others or to himself. The facts are: he has no record of anti-social behavior, he suffered a trauma and a period of rest and healing might be all that is necessary for him to live a healthy and productive life. He's twenty-three," the bearded Dr. Middleton said, resting now calm and contented like an old lion on a rock ledge just after having roared.

"I see," the psychologist said, sharpening her voice. "And you, Mr. Anderson? Do you believe Donald Wallis is responding favorably to therapy?"

"Yes, Doctor, a rapid response to therapy. He is demonstrating empathy and sensitivity to others. A positive response, Doctor."

"Yes," the psychologist said. "Well, then. We shall keep this patient here for continued observation and evaluation, Mr. Anderson. Shall we say, two weeks? Medication remains the same. Fine. You are dismissed from this hearing and placed under Mr. Anderson's care. Donald Wallis, you are assigned to the Open Ward for the next two weeks. Do you understand?"

I nodded with a minimum of understanding.

"Yes," I said.

I looked back over my shoulder at Mr. Anderson who motioned for me to rise, which I did, and he escorted me to the door and to the nurse who walked me out into the Open Ward.

The psychologist wanted to put me in Camarillo, a State mental hospital, where I could have been confined for years, or forever.

Come on.

It went well, I thought.

Did it?

~~~

The larger patient population spread out comfortably between the small Locked Ward I had just left and the even smaller padded room where I didn't want to go. Unlike the Locked Ward and the Solitary Room, there were always two or more staff people present. A nurse on the staff brought us our food, our water and our pills. I didn't talk to her that first day except for: "Thank you, Nurse."

~~~

I felt better sitting in a single chair off by myself looking out one of the larger windows. I stayed there most of the day, leaning my head into my right hand and using it to hold my head up.

Like an actor on stage, I watched and listened.

It felt good to have a wall of air between me and the other patients who were all on the other side of the room.

I ate again and waited for visiting hour. My eyebrows tingled and I had a lump in my throat.

~~~

Jim looked cheerful. Roberta acted friendly. And Mom looked worried. She was quiet.

I looked at my mother's scared-looking face for a second and lowered my head ashamed, and overtaken by how much.

"Hi," I said. "Mom…"

"Jim and Roberta brought me in their little car. I've been worried-sick. I haven't been able to sleep. They wouldn't let me see you: the hospital. I would have come."

"Yeah," I said. "Sure. I know, Mom."

"Are you all right?"

"Better," I nodded. "I got to sit by a window back over there today."

"Are they giving you enough to eat? I brought you a chopped egg sandwich, some oatmeal cookies and an apple."

"Thanks," I said, taking the sandwich out of the brown bag and out of the wax paper and biting into it right away.

"It's one of your favorites, right," Mom said. "Is it good?"

"Un huh," I mumbled, gobbling the cool chopped egg sandwich down like a starving dog. The little mustard and the fats in the mayonnaise were absolutely delicious.

"You look good," Roberta said.

They were watching me eat fast. So was I. Surprisingly without biting my fingers.

"I don't want to go back there, Guys."

"He won't have to, will he? Berkeley?" Mom asked Jim.

"The Locked Ward," I said, trying to communicate what I had meant.

"You're in the Open Ward now, Don," Jim said. "But it'll be better if you stay here for a while. They'll cut your meds back too, in time."

"They don't hurt people here," Roberta said. "Or punish them for drawing or writing."

42

"Or try to stop you from being who you are," Jim said. "I'll phone Ed in Palo Alto and some of your friends here."

"Ed?" I repeated. Ed's face was coming into focus slowly.

"Don?" Jim said.

"Okay, Jim."

"I don't want any of those Berkeley people hurting him again," Mom said.

"Ed helped me, Mom. Didn't he, Jim?"

"Yes, he did, Mrs. Wallis."

"Well, I don't know."

"And Mr. Anderson and Dr. Middleton," I said. "The psychologist wanted to send me to Camarillo."

"Dr. Middleton delivered you when you were born."

"He did?"

"At General," Mom said. "Not in Psycho."

"Psycho?" I repeated, feeling something rigid move across through the inside of my stomach.

"No one's sending you to Camarillo," Jim said. "You can check yourself out when you want, Don. Remember that. And you can stay at your mom's, or at our place when you get out."

"Out?" I asked.

~~~

"Your turn, Don," Mr. Anderson said.

We called Mr. Anderson Dennis in and out of group. We sat in a circle. Each patient spoke in turn.

"Fine, I guess," I said, wondering what I should say next.

"Fine?" he quoted me, questioningly.

"Uh huh," I said.

"How are visits going?" he asked.

"Good," I said, and nodded. "My mom brings me sandwiches and cookies from home."

"And your dad, Don? Have you heard from him?"

"He's up north in Tacoma," I said. "He's not well. Mom said she phoned him long distance to Washington the other night, but she didn't say much. And he said even less, she said. Anyway, he can't come right now, because he's sick."

43

"And how do you feel about that?"
"I don't."

~~~

My brother Milo said something, or I did. He wasn't really
supportive of the Vietnam War, but he wasn't really against it either.
He had a heart murmur that kept him from being drafted. He dropped
out of Junior College and got a job driving a laundry delivery truck all
over the county. He said our thirteen-year old brother Johnny Lee had
shown an interest in joining Cadets at the public high school. I asked
Milo why Mom and he hadn't talked Johnny out of it. It was a
program to prepare boys for the military, wasn't it? Milo started
condemning draft dodgers, dope users and hippies. I accused Mom
and Milo of being too passive to stand up against the government.
Milo said he knew he wasn't a dummy. I asked him what that meant.
Then he said, "At least I'm not the one in Psycho." And then I said,
"I'm not the one who belongs in a mental health clinic. You are." We
stopped talking and he left.

~~~

"Thoughts are one thing," Dennis Anderson said, "but feelings are
another. Thoughts go across the screen in our heads. Most ideas
come in from the outside and go right back out. But we live with our
feelings. The ones that have burrowed deep down inside don't come
out easily. We'll teach you some tools you can use. Logic can help to
process ideas. And tears and laughter can help to release the feelings
you have which are attached to your thoughts."

~~~

"This is your final evaluation, Mr. Wallis," the psychologist said.
    I nodded.
    She waited.
    "Yes," I said.
    "Mr. Anderson says you are progressing very well in group."
    I waited.
    "Are you still resentful of authority, rebellious and even hostile to
society? Are you?"
    "I don't want to hurt anymore, Doctor."
    "What about other people, Mr. Wallis?"

44

"I don't want anybody to be hurt."

"Really!" she exclaimed.

"I don't want to hurt anyone."

"All right, Mr. Wallis. You'll be an outpatient for at least two-and-a-half months. You are to report to the Clinic Monday through Friday to Mr. Anderson's afternoon therapy group."

"Yes. Thank you."

"But before you leave, Don, you should know and accept that you're never going to amount to anything. So, you might as well get yourself a janitor job and write your poetry as a hobby in your spare time."

The hurt I felt hearing her say that to me grew up so fast through fire that it hit the back wall of ice before I could breathe or blink an eyelash.

"Is that it?" I asked.

"Yes."

~~~

I didn't like the psychologist saying that. So, to be honest, I guess, I knew there was a chance she might be right.

My normal talking was improving rapidly. But complicated thinking, feeling, comprehending, reading and writing were still too difficult. It would continue to be. And it seemed like I'd never be able to memorize lines and act on stage again even though it seemed like I was acting all the time now whether I was around other people, or not.

~~~

I had some cheap pens, ruled paper and a broken binder full of poems.

I tried to write down what I was thinking, and how I felt, but the few words and phrases I did come up with didn't work well. I started but it would take me forty years to complete the project. Thoughts of famous writers such as Steinbeck and Hemingway floated like momentary buoys toward the horizon in my mind: the Caribbean, the Pacific, and the Atlantic. And I lived a simple life, aspiring to do great things. But my writing left me sick and chilled a little: somehow cold and anxious at the same time.

~~~

I wondered if anyone would trust me after my nervous breakdown. I didn't. I felt different. A lot of my mind seemed permanently lost, and what was left seemed drugged and hushed.

I constantly forgot it was the Thorazine slowing me down. More than one friend of mine over the years had to remind me that I lived in a sick world and, knowing it, I had had an appropriate response. Stuck between putting my body on a railroad track to stop the troop trains in Oakland or joining the Weathermen and learning how to make bombs, I flipped the switch because my heart could not choose to commit suicide or to kill anyone. I was now a minority surrounded by an ill majority who were living in ignorance and denial. So, my question should not be why did I have a nervous breakdown, but why didn't more people have one?

The Selective Service System sent me a medical discharge. They were through with me as it turned out.

~~~

I married Rena in March.

In May, a year after the Alameda Sheriff deputies killed James Rector and blinded Alan Blanchard at People's Park in Berkeley, I saw the photo of the shrieking girl kneeling next to the body of Jeffrey Miller at Kent State on the front page of the L.A. Times. The Ohio National Guard had opened fire on campus after one of their younger members panicked and started firing his loaded rifle.

I was holding the unfolded newspaper in my hands.

I seemed to remember Rena had a friend she went to high school with on Long Island who was going to school in Ohio at Kent State. I wound up asking her what her friend's name was, and if she had seen the newspapers? I had to tell her, her friend Jeffrey Miller had been killed. She started crying and I watched and listened while I waited for her to be able to talk. Miller was a smiling kid, she told me. They played chess together lots of times but he never joined S.D.S. like she did. And I said I was sorry.

~~~

I shared with Dennis Anderson that I was worried about not remembering a lot of what happened before my breakdown. He

46

assured me that much of my memory would come back over time, and what did not wouldn't matter. He was preparing me to face the future.

~~~

I had no idea how much I needed to learn. I just knew I still wanted to learn it.

~~~

I also knew I was me, whoever that was.

But according to the laws of the theater, like a character in a story, play or movie, I was either a common character in an unusual situation or an uncommon character in a normal situation and I knew it. What I didn't know yet was that like many other people I was my own greatest obstacle and most powerful opposition. I was my own worst enemy. And even though I had lost much of my memory and the speed of my mental and physical abilities, I could feel and I felt overwhelmed, betrayed, defeated and deserted.

Call me Slow, Lethargic, Snail, Slug or Over-Emotional Sloth. Call me Hodge Podge like the kids in high school did. Call me Hodge. Call me Outsider, Rebel, Creative-And-Egotistical, Yellow, Coward, Traitor, The Good Kid or The Shy-Kid-With-The-Problem. Call me Appleseed. Call me Country Bumpkin. Call me a fool and an idiot.

I was still hurt and angry and recovering.

I was grieving.

~~~

Eventually I wanted to study Russian and Rena wanted to study Chinese. We wanted to study History, Philosophy, Literature and Religions… cultures… to help bring peace through the United Nations and international education to the world. But working in the theater was the only place I knew of in America where a young man could express a wide range of emotion. Acting, writing and drawing helped me to confront myself and other people. I needed to learn how to live with my thoughts and feelings—and theirs. The Theater, Literature and Art offered a world and a place for me to live in.

One of the many good things I experienced was getting to see the poet and translator Kenneth Rexroth at a memorial for Pablo Neruda who had died a week after Neruda's friend Allende was assassinated in Chile.

I also met the politicized actors of Teatro de La Esperanza in Santa Barbara and on campus. Their theater, a grandchild of the San Francisco Mime Troupe and Luis Valdez's Teatro des Los Campesinos, eventually toured the Americas, Europe and the Soviet Union.

~~~

I wrote a long multimedia one-act play called *Our Minimum Wage* and performed it one evening as a Readers' Theater on campus. It was about my experiences working with my mother at a sweatshop laundry in San Luis Obispo right after high school. My Aunt Helen drove my mom down for the performance.

~~~

I've walked a mile, or more, and gone back up to my room. Bright sun. My head is hot and dripping wet with sweat.

I'm worrying.

I'm going to the restroom to use cold water and paper towels to lower my temperature. I'm placing wet towels around my warm wrists and on my hot forehead. I'm looking in the mirror and seeing how distraught I look. I look frightened and desperate. I'm starting to cry and to make whimpering sounds like a small naked child walking blindly down a road leading away from the mushroom cloud above and behind her in Hiroshima or Nagasaki... or the napalm in Vietnam. But, obviously, my simile is inappropriate. Figuring that out, I calm down and start to breathe normally again.

~~~

My head hurt. My mind was swelling up against the inside of my skull. I was overheated. There was a dry taste in my mouth. All the muscles in my chest, in my whole body, were contracting. It was like my eyes were set in hard concrete and some kind of electricity was sizzling through my joints. I was burning... And the back of my head felt like a falling bomb that was going to explode any second.

I thought I was having another breakdown.

~~~

I told Rena to divorce me. And I got her to do it.

~~~

My youngest brother Johnny Lee and our cousin David Lee drove down to Isla Vista and evacuated me before I totally lost it. I was twenty-seven years old.

John was planning to join the Air Force: Death from Above. I knew he had been thinking about it, but I didn't know he had already talked Mom into signing him into the Service early.

~~~

1974.

Green January hills surround San Luis Obispo. The cowtown I had fled in the middle 1960s had grown into a safe and secure little place far from the fast pace of the world.

There are trees everywhere. The trees are mounted like large sculptures along very quiet streets. Unique wooden houses have orange and lemon trees in their front yards. The people I see are all ages: grandparents, parents and children. There are families here, and not just an over-population of college students like in Isla Vista at U.C.S.B.

There is little or no pressure.

Two weeks back home and I feel a whole lot better. I'm even starting to think that I may enjoy the future.

~~~

Minute by minute, month by month, I learned to laugh at myself a little and then how to make fun of everyone.

I founded the San Luis Obispo County Portable Theatre, worked with nearly thirty actors and produced sixteen or more street theatre skits. Our biggest audiences were during the Abalone Alliance's anti-Diablo Canyon Nuclear Power Plant blockade. We were a good educational tool and inspiration for social action. We reached thousands of people and helped them to stand up for themselves. Other skits dealt with feminist issues, the plight of minimum wage workers and the inhuman practice of capital punishment.

~~~

After two and a half years I missed performing more legitimate theatre and got permission from Friar Tuck's Refectory in downtown San Luis Obispo to use their Hofbrau lunch room for an intimate theater on Friday and Saturday nights and for rehearsals Monday through Thursday nights.

My name was on thirty-six of the thirty-seven Off-Broadway/West's one-act productions. I produced, directed and acted. Directing such actors as the Swedish-trained Einar Berg, the very experienced Thelma Anderson and the naturally talented Michael McLarney added greatly to my knowledge and understanding of acting. I always tried to stretch my actors' experience with newer and more demanding roles for them and myself.

We did two of my plays: *The Blind Man* based on the artist Alan Blanchard being blinded at People's Park in Berkeley and another about my parents and I. Inspired by Jerzi Grotowski's *Poor Theatre* in Poland, I greatly condensed and altered several classic plays to fifteen to forty-five minutes in length, with five or less roles. Projects included the ancient Greek playwright Euripedes' *Medea*, Shakespeare's *Macbeth* and the Spanish novelist Cervantes' *Don Quixote*. Performing Robert Louis Stevenson's insane *Dr. Jekyll and Mr. Hyde* and the transitions between the man's dual personalities in front of a small intimate audience was the most challenging psychological role I ever played. It was also the closest attempt that I had yet made to confess that I had been mentally ill. I had small audiences and a little of their understanding.

Joanna Verhaar was my partner through most of the Off-Broadway/West years. She was a secretary in the Child Development Department at Cal Poly and a family and marriage counselor who later established her full-time practice.

Quite often I would still stare into a bathroom mirror until I sensed how I really felt and watched myself cry. Many's the time I fell on a bed, curled up into a fetal position and shed tears while my body shook… from twice a day to only once or twice a season over the next ten to forty years.

~~~

I continued doing comedies to keep working on feeling better—and dramas to express my social criticism.

I was at my peak: performing one production while rehearsing another and preparing yet another for production. We staged a new production every six to eight weeks. We all excelled and continued working for nearly three years. With such obsession and stress on my part, perhaps I was ready for an early stroke or a heart attack but the restaurant lost its lease and we lost our theater space.

Portable Theatre had gotten as far as Ukiah in Northern California. Off-Broadway/West never quite made it to Los Angeles. My experience however had grown immensely. I had produced and directed over sixty shows and played over a hundred roles on stage and radio (KCBX and KCPR).

A year later my dad died.

~~~

I remembered Dad seemed more comfortable around grown-up men and women than he did with us kids or other people's children. He told few jokes and even fewer stories but he smiled and sang Mom, Milo and me songs he learned in the 1930s and 40s. I liked singing with him and singing his songs when he wasn't with me. The one I liked the most, I guess, was Mr. Leadbetter's song, *Goodnight, Irene*.

> "Irene, goodnight… Irene,
> I'll see you in my dreams."

~~~

Dad was one of the youngest kids in a large family during the Depression. His older brothers and sisters (most of whom were married and already had their own families) were all living at home. His dad was the only one out of the whole bunch who had a job. Grandfather Wallis worked at a Post Office in Ohio but he didn't make enough money to feed them all. One morning Dad's mother came out of the kitchen and stared hard at everyone in the living room. "There are too many people here," she said. "You can't all stay. So, who's going to leave?" She looked around the room like she was looking for volunteers but everyone lowered their eyes to avoid her face, everyone except my dad. He didn't take his eyes off her the whole time. Eventually her eyes landed on him.

That night he slipped out an upstairs window, got down the side and left. Just turned eleven and before sun up the very next morning he jumped his first freight. He spent the next three years on and off trains, traveling with other hobos all over the West. He would go from Ohio to Washington to California, back around to see his parents and then leave again. He buddied up with older guys he liked and trusted, and learned from them how to walk around to the backdoor of a farmhouse and knock on the door and ask the farmwoman for work. He'd say, "I'd gladly do any chores you need done, ma'am, for a potato or a carrot I could make a soup out of, thank you."

He joined the Civilian Conservation Corps and worked with hundreds of other young guys up in the Northwest building bridges over the wild rivers and making trails through the mountain pine forests. They lived in white canvas tents in huge camps high up in the Cascade and Sierra mountain ranges of Washington, Oregon and Northern California. He joined the Old Army (U.S.) when he turned sixteen. When he finished his four years of service, WWII broke out so he reenlisted and followed General MacArthur through the jungles of Borneo and New Guinea, back through the Philippines and into Japan.

~~~

I watch him drink beer out of a bottle, without a glass, at the tavern nearest to where we live. I sit on a stool next to him at the counter. It's okay for me to go in with him because it's officially a cafe because they serve heated sandwiches. Dad holds some of the cold, watery beer against his unbrushed green-stained teeth before he swallows all of it. The cold beer burns the inside of his mouth and throat. I know this because he has given me a sip. It smells. In a way, it stinks.

I lean up against the bulbous jukebox in the tavern. I'm just tall enough to read the song titles and the performers' names through the shining colored lights underneath the glass. Hank Snow. Tex Ritter. Red Foley and Miss Kitty Wells. I sing along with the records. I'm getting a strawberry soda and potato chips from the heavyset man at the bar. Dad grinned when the man bet me a nine-year old boy couldn't sound like a grown-up. I started practicing when I was five or six.

"…goodnight, Irene.
I'll see you in my dreams."

~~~

52

I wrote. And I grieved. I continued to grieve for myself, my dad and all the men and women who had ever lived.

Losing my dad led me back to my childhood—and my grieving led me to my deepest feelings and made my motivation for having heart-to-hearts with people and for working in the written, visual and performing arts only more sincere and honest.

~~~

I performed one-man shows of Mark Twain periodically for eight years. That was a good experience. Twain was smart, sensitive and extremely funny. He was also deeply hurt, and angry.

~~~

I was about thirty-three years old and living in the rear of an old garage and broke. I had done a lot of work and still showed potential so the sad joke was—after sixteen years—when would I get it together and make something work.

Trying to forget the question, I shelved my unsuccessful and unfinished writing projects and took two weeks off. After I got some fresh sea air, I started thinking about puppets… and I didn't stop thinking about puppets for the next thirty years.

~~~

I'm looking at a photo of the eighty-four-year-old Chinese People's Puppet Master Tsien Tsia-chu. He is wearing metal rim glasses, a wrapped cloth turban and a thick tunic. He has a white mustache and a small beard. He is looking at a small wooden puppet head he is holding close to his chest, a hand-carving tool in his right hand. He looks like he's concentrating although he appears to be relaxed. His head and hands look slender, strong and flexible. He looks like a calm elderly artisan with a rich interior life. He looks like a friendly man I would enjoy meeting.

The photo is in a slender book: J.T. MacDermott's translation of a chapter from the Russian puppeteer Sergei Obraztsov's book *The Chinese Theatre*. Obraztsov is quite clear about the Chinese puppeteers knowing that the whole body and arms make the expressive gestures needed on stage.

~~~

Puppetry has been an art on every continent on earth for 35,000 to 70,000 years. It is one of the most wondrous art forms human beings have ever practiced. Ancient puppets represented the spirits and beings people believed were involved in their lives. A modern puppet character shows us our neighbors and ourselves. They do this with their appearance and actions. A good puppet comes alive and says what people are thinking but not saying out loud.

~~~

I plan ahead and then carve from the larger shapes to the smaller details.

I make my puppet heads 3" to 3½" in diameter: which is much larger than the Chinese hand puppets' heads. I also make my puppets' hands larger (the size of the faces); and I attach a dowel at the wrists. I make a strong cuff that I sew to the dowel on each hand. The dowel is the puppet's forearm, and is shaped to fit my thumb or my little finger on my left or right hand (since I do not use my middle finger which is stronger than my little finger but does not make the puppets look as well proportioned). This requires me to know ahead of time which hand the puppet will go on: my left or my right. The decision is based on which side of the stage the puppet will be on in the script. It also requires me to exercise and strengthen my little fingers.

~~~

I carve the shape of the eyes and the lines in a puppet's forehead and around its eyes and mouth to express the middle range of its character so that it will read believably for all the emotions it will express during the play.

~~~

"What are you doing?" my Wolfie puppet asked in his Count Dracula voice.

"Trying to remember how I carve puppets."

"You forgot?"

"I'm trying to figure the best way to tell someone else how to do it," I said.

"Who?" he demanded.

"Whoever's interested," I said.

"Well," Wolfie said, "the woodcarver must carve the wood with the heart of a toymaker." He sighed.

"Wolfie?"

Giving me a look before he pretended to ignore me for a while, he said, "You saw a rectangular basswood block. Woodcarvers call it a blank. You draw the profile of the head or the hands on the sides, pad the areas that will become the ears with cloth and put it into a vise. You use sharp chisels. Two: a one-inch and a half-inch. You use the big one to carve the larger areas first, and the smaller one to carve the finer details last. You carve with the grain. You never point the sharp chisel, and absolutely never a dull one, at yourself."

Wolfie shook his head.

He stopped talking. It looked like he was wiping tears out of his eyes with his front paws. He sucked his tears in-between his teeth.

"Wolfie?" I asked.

Wolfie sniffled the nostrils on his big wet snout.

He howled mournfully, and neither of us spoke until he said, "Hunters. One morning in Siberia... my right-paw was bleeding and the blood was freezing. My mother put a Band-Aid on it. She put a quilt of rabbit furs in bed all around me."

~~~

The puppeteer should not move the puppet without a reason. Find a reason, and then move the puppet appropriately.

With the energy and enthusiasm of a life-long performer, the English puppeteer Jan Bussell wrote, "The most important thing is for you yourself to feel the part. If you make yourself feel angry, or glad or sad, your puppet is likely to do the same. It can be very hard work feeling all the emotions that all the puppets you handle have to experience. But it is exciting, and very necessary to their success."

Empathy. Empathy. Empathy...

I'll add that everything to do with puppetry is important but some things will be more important than others relative to the puppeteer, the time, the place and the audience. Like life, theatre is an art in constant change. Relax, and enjoy it. It will take practice and experience to become familiar with the many things and parts of it and their varying relevance. And remember to take care of the puppeteer—yourself—because ultimately it is you, the performer, who is the show.

~~~

I flipped Gunter Bohmer's small book *The Wonderful World of Puppets* open to the marked page showing the black and white photo of an 18th/19th century Japanese netsuke carving of a beaming puppeteer performing a hand puppet show in front of his chest with one of the small children in his audience delightfully reaching up to the side of his shoulder-hung box theater. They both looked absolutely happy and alive.

I looked at the photo often for support, inspiration and pride.

~~~

"Men," my mom said.

I relived stepping outside to get away from her. The screen door slammed shut behind me but it didn't stop her from shouting. I hurried to the far end of the backyard to help my father who was usually good-natured for the longest time when he was drinking.

"Mom's pretty upset, Dad," I said, coming up behind him while he bent down to pick the grill for the barbecue pit up off the ground. I saw him grab the grill and raise it up and drop it. He bent all the way down again to pick it back up. It seemed strange that he was fumbling and dropping something physical like that. I saw him mumbling. Saliva foamed up between his lips.

"Mom sure is angry," I said. Dad dropped the grill again. I heard him panting hard when he bent down the third time to get it. "She's shouting at me to clean my room and do stuff. But I'm not going to do it until she stops shouting," I said, watching him get a hold of the grill and drop it again. Bent over and staggering in place, he fumbled with his belt buckle. Bobbing, he grabbed the buckle and pulled his whole belt out of his Levis with his right hand and then grabbed the end of it with his left hand.

Dad's six feet four inches sprang up and around like a massive uncoiling spring lashing upward and outward from the ground: a catapult.

"You'll do what she tells you to do," he shouted on his way up, swinging the metal belt buckle at me hard across the side of my face.

~~~

Six years later, Dad told me, "You'll have many fathers in your life, Son. But you'll only have one mother." Saying that to me was both a cop out on the one hand, I now realize, and a profound piece of wisdom on the other considering he left home on his own at eleven and learned what he needed to know from older hobos: men other than his father.

~~~

When I remembered my nervous breakdown I'd start to worry about being sick again. I'd take a walk, or focus on making something… a costume, a wig, a prop… or on talking to someone, a heart-to-heart, or on writing… and my mood would change for a while as my thoughts and actions did, from heavy to lighter. The changes usually occurred more easily, but not always.

I often felt lonely and sad.

I wanted to be in a safe open place, and be my old self again. But most of what I was interested in—museums, libraries, universities, theaters, galleries and publishers—were far away in New York City and San Francisco, or the large cities in Europe and Asia… and I still felt I had to be quite courageous just to travel alone to San Jose or Bakersfield.

What I needed the most, I think, was to know that I was surrounded by friends whenever I wasn't working at my easel, worktable, puppet stage or desk. I wanted to be a creative person and to love and be loved. But I was all too well aware of how I had let my friends and loved ones down. All my life, I had failed in so many ways… so many times.

~~~

I was mending some canvas sails for a small pirate ship when my puppet Little Boy showed up.

"Want to help me?" I asked. "I've got some large needles and carpet thread here in the sewing kit."

"Mothers sew," he said. "Boys don't sew. Pirates don't."

"Buoys don't," I said, "but pirates do." Then, changing from my normal voice to my Captain Long John Silver voice, I said, "Shiver my timbers, Matey. Do you want to play pirates, Little Boy? Or do

57

you want to play spaceship with cyborgs taking green-tinted mice to the moon to eat the cheese?"

Little Boy looked deep into my face, not moving an eyelash.

I continued my heavy-voiced interrogation. "Ben Gunn on Treasure Island, he likes cheese. You want to be Ben Gunn and live like a wild and crazy pirate alone with only goats on a deserted island? Well, do ya, Little Boy?"

I could tell I had fallen overboard but I couldn't quite stop myself even though I could see that Little Boy was starting to get upset.

"Pirates," he said. He acted out, gesturing with his arm as if he was fighting with a sword. "Pirates: firing their cannons and slashing the enemy with their swords."

Leaning closer to him, I said, "The smoke from the cannons lashing their faces and blinding their eyes."

"Huh?" he said, looking dumbfounded.

"Their blood burning off the flaming surface of the wooden decks," I continued. "Their guts oozing out of their abdomens, charbroiled in the flames."

"You're messing it up," he said. "You're not playing."

"Yes, I am," I said. "It's different when grown-ups do it."

"I know," he said and stepped away. "You're making it all up."
He shook his head, turned his back and walked away.

"Whoops," I said.

~~~

"Ouch!" I screamed, raising and lowering my left hand several times while I danced around in place. I raised the pulsating pain in my thumb into my mouth and sucked on it like a little boy.

"Are you dancing to a sea chantey?" my puppet Red asked.

I opened my eyes and saw the sharp point of the needle.

Red was examining me.

I leaned into her face and said in my Long John Silver voice, "No. Remember we're friends, Red. You can trust me."

"Can I wear a pirate's costume?" she asked. "Like Little Boy?"
"Huh?"

"He's going to have a costume," she said.

"Well," I started to say.

"I want a scarlet silk blouse with puffy sleeves, black cotton pants, black leather boots, a black wide-brimmed hat, a white lace scarf and a black silk sash, gold earrings and a real pearl necklace," Red said. "Okay?"

I pulled Red close and hugged her.

The kids want pirates, I thought.

"We will make you the best costume any lady pirate has ever worn on the high seas," I said.

She smiled.

And for a moment I knew my heart was a treasure chest and I was holding all the wealth in the world.

~~~

I studied puppetry books Ken Hall sent me from Europe. Thanks to Dr. Michael Malkin, I found others in the rare books collection at the Cal Poly library. I learned what I could about how to carve wooden puppets from woodworking magazines and later from the members of the California Woodcarvers Guild located in San Simeon.

After I practiced for a year, Marvin Lee went with me to the Downtown SLO Thursday Night Farmers' Market in January 1984. I started on the corner of Garden and Higuera Streets. I gathered audiences and held their attention for nine to eighteen minutes at a time. Then I passed the hat.

I did five or six shows a night, forty-five Thursday nights a year, up and down Higuera Street in San Luis Obispo for the next ten years and once or twice a month for another sixteen years. I performed on the weekends at the Nipomo Swap Meet for twenty-three years. I performed at nearby fairs, at California Living Museum (CALM) along the Kern River near Bakersfield and at Art fairs in old-town Monterey near Fishermen's Wharf. I also went to an Earth Day celebration at U.C. Davis where I heard Bishop Desmond Tutu from South Africa speak, to Danish Day celebrations in the Hans Christian Andersen community of Solvang and to dozens of schools between Santa Ynez and San Miguel.

Eventually the San Luis Obispo County Health Department asked me to apply for a grant to use State anti-tobacco funds to do educational outreach in the community. I wrote three scripts and reached over thirty-seven-thousand people at fairs and in the schools throughout the county during the twenty-month program.

~~~

Ken Hall photographed my early puppets and helped me keep up my morale. He got me four of Walter Wilkinson's books about his annual summer jaunts with his hand puppets through different areas of Britain during the 1930s. Einar Berg donated countless hours taking professional photos of my puppets; there were lots of photographs, newspaper clippings and souvenirs; and many German and Japanese tourists made videos of my shows especially the first fifteen years.

~~~

Because my younger brothers were married and had children, I stayed with my mother and nursed her for several months after her heart by-pass operation. In the hospital she whispered so softly I couldn't hear her. When I put my ear to her mouth I finally heard her ask for ice in a cloth to moisten her lips. She said they were burning. When she came home, I fixed her elegant and costly meals three times a day and served her fine foods she had never had before.

Unable to work any more, Mom met Al Mazza at a senior lunch, became his friend and eventually married him. Their relationship was a Cinderella story and she enjoyed leisure, travel and affection for ten years before she died.

~~~

Memories of my childhood on the small Manteca farm and the large apple ranch near York Mountain Winery reminded me of how much I loved being with my family in the great outdoors. We were always looking after each other and helping each other to do things. And thinking of my dad too again and all the trips we took across Northern California and the Great Northwest inspired me to take my wooden hand puppets to families who were recreating and playing in the State Parks.

~~~

August is family month in the California State Parks. I experienced families wanting to be mellow, to get in touch with their inner selves and to really be with each other.

I was proud of the shows at Montana de Oro and Morro Bay State Parks. At the 11:00 Sunday morning shows in Morro Bay State Park I used my smaller Japanese-style in-front-of-my-chest booth. Large crowds of families sat on benches or stood close beside each other. They allowed themselves to be themselves, to be together and to relax. My puppets were eager to do the rest.

I did a hundred-and-twenty performances in the parks.

~~~

Switching from Mark Twain, I performed one-man shows of John Muir's material many times from wilderness campsites all over San Luis Obispo County to Juvenile Hall. Muir's writings helped me to appreciate wildness in nature and to bear the loss and deaths of many people I cared about.

~~~

My large John Muir rod puppet sat back in his pale green-blue chair, wearing his old hat, before the totally attentive forty teenage kids in the County Juvenile Hall. I talked for him in my softer Scottish accent.

"The most important duty I have set for myself is to get as near the heart of the world as I can. All the sun shines on is beautiful, so long as it is wild. Every day opens and closes like a flower, noiseless, effortless. Divine peace glows on all the majestic landscape, like the silent enthusiastic joy that sometimes transfigures a noble human face… Earth has no sorrow that earth cannot heal. All scars she heals, whether in rocks or water or sky or the human heart."

~~~

Mom died in 1995.

~~~

I remembered my mom was born on a flat cotton and potato farm in Wasco over in the Valley near Shafter and Bakersfield.

She had to start working in her mother's kitchen by the age of three. She could barely reach the top of the stove so she had to stand on a wooden box. The door on the wood burning stove was heavy so she had to use both hands and arms to pull it down to look in on the roasts, breads and pies like little Gretel in the fairy tale. She sometimes had to cook for a dozen workers (big adults) whom her father had hired to help with the harvests—and for her nine brothers and sisters. She told me she once burned her father's supper and it tasted terrible. Her dad took one taste, she said. He glanced at her and without saying a word he finished eating every bite on his plate and thanked her for fixing it. She felt horrible for letting him down. Mom never ruined another meal for him or anyone else for the rest of her life.

Catholic nuns at her school taught my mother arithmetic and how to read and write. She learned the basics. But her penmanship was beautiful. She was an artist at it. Her schooling only lasted until her sophomore year of High School but, of course, even before then she never went to school when she was needed at home: in the house or out in the field. Many years later, in-between her endless chores, she would sit down in her kitchen and teach me how to form my letters and practice my penmanship.

I can still imagine her as a small child at the age of five back in Wasco pulling a hundred pound cotton sack. I can almost feel her pulling it to keep up with her father. I see the cotton burr cuts and the blood on her fingers. I see her small face the first time she thinks she has lost him. She's out in the middle of the field searching the white wall of cotton all around her to find the sweat on the back of his tan shirt, to grab the red handkerchief that hung from inside his right hip pocket or to smell the cheap cigar smoke buried in the brim of his old gray hat. She could only see the dumb inhuman dirt at her feet and the deaf empty blue sky ahead of her eyes. I can feel her stretching her neck, locking her knees and digging her toes into the dirt to anchor her spine in the earth before the scream she was screaming burst out of her throat.

~~~

Mom is walking back and forth around the plot the men have lowered her father's casket into. I feel her avoiding the dirt, the ground and the headstones. She keeps her chin raised high and her feet moving. She's searching for her father as if he is above ground somewhere at the cemetery. She glares at the tallest trees and the highest peaks of the hills in the clear blue sky. I can almost feel her blunted, frustrated rage crash against the outer walls of her first initial tears.

It's all right, Mom... I say to myself. It's all right.

~~~

In 1996, I took my partner Nancy and some puppets to Europe. We only had the stewardesses to offer us guidance and they were offering me way too much French wine.

Me: a fifty year-old country bumpkin. Scared and elated, I raced my mind in all directions: backward over all my life and dreams and forward over the mountains and prairies of North America toward Hudson Bay and the ice and water of the North Atlantic Ocean and beyond toward the land of my mother's ancestors.

~~~

I first thought the cloud formations, the bodies of snow and ice and the vast expanse of chilling choppy water looked huge. Big seemed to shrink though compared to the bigness of the sky and the cosmos. I was a nearly insignificant speck of consciousness confined to a slightly solid mass of matter that rarely seemed as real as the story I had been telling in my head.

~~~

Leaning toward the window, Nancy and I saw the small groves of trees, the pastures and the simple farmhouses and barns that led to the French international airport of Orly-Sud.

~~~

We took a shuttle bus into the outskirts of Paris and then the train to Metro Odeon.

Constantly in a state of repair, the Hotel Stella, which was built on the14th century wall of the old city, had a concierge but no televisions, elevators or breakfast service. Our double room had two windows over-looking a narrow courtyard with a few trees and actual laundry drying on clotheslines.

Too excited to rest, we went out and down the narrow streets to Notre Dame. We found les bouguinistes, the old green booths of used-books, prints and postcards along the banks of the river Seine, the Place St. Michel (a fountain sculpture where members of the Resistance shot it out with WWII German soldiers) and then Notre Dame. I actually liked the smaller church on the side and the trees and the lamp streetlights that started to come on at sunset more than the interior of the larger cathedral which was dark and felt like a crypt.

Walking back, like a couple of kids, we got a banana split with European ice cream and real whipped cream at a cafe.

We stopped at the Creamerie Restaurant Polidor next to the Hotel Stella to get a simple meal of poulet et legumes (chicken and peas). We ordered une carafe d'eau (a carafe of tap water) and no wine. The place had lace curtains in the front window and tiny wooden drawers where regulars stored their linen napkins. It had been there since 1845. Older university people sat elbow to elbow at long narrow tables. Some of the Polidor's specials were written in chalk on a blackboard. In the past, struggling writers like Verlaine, Joyce, Valery and Hemingway had been regulars. Years later, we would discover that the contemporary American novelist Richard Ford loved the Polidor as well. They served great home style cooking and we had a real citrus lemon tart for dessert.

I don't know if the American novelist Richard Wright, who wrote *Black Boy* and *Native Son*, ever ate there. But he lived in the neighborhood and Martin Luther King, Jr. visited him there in the late 1950s.

~~~

We explored the older city of Paris on foot. We watched uniformed children walking single file like little ducks on the sidewalk to school through the large windows of a coffee bar we stopped at for espressos and croissants for breakfast. Then we continued our walk on to *Musée du Louvre* where we stood eye-to-eye with Leonardo da Vinci's unclean small 21x30" painting of the *Mona Lisa* only because we were taller than the hundreds of people standing in front of us. I stood in awe before Gericault's large painting of the *Raft of the Medusa* showing the suffering but impassioned survivors of a shipwreck watching a ship that could have saved them disappear out of sight... and at the boy and others in Delacroix's *Liberty Leading the People*. We walked around Michelangelo's sculpture of the *Dying Slave* and the anonymous Greek sculptor's *Venus de Milo*. And finally in the Egyptian Antiquities we saw the 4,400 year old, less than eighteen inches tall, wooden sculpture of a man and a woman holding hands as they walk forward into the future. A portrait of humanity, I thought. A masterpiece, it commanded my stillness and held my attention. It still does.

~~~

Our immediate future led us outdoors to rest and smile while we watched the children and their parents sail boats with multicolored sails, catching the wind, on the ponds in the *Jardins des Tuileries*.

Another day we visited the *Theatre des Marionettes du Jardin du Luxembourg*, Paris's largest puppet theater, a bare building next to the wooden animal merry-go-round and the fenced-in play area in the park in back of the *Musée Rodin*. One of the staff rang a bell to get the children and their parents to line up for the show. Guignol (hand puppet or marionette) is the national puppet of France. To the south was the City of Lyon where the puppet Guignol was born out of the creative imagination of one man and the very real needs of an entire community of oppressed and hungry but hardworking people: the silk weavers of Lyon.

We sat with the parents close behind the children so I could at least watch them responding to what was happening on stage. As the show began, Guignol entered the stage with his long black pigtail and long Chinese-style coat and all the French children screamed, "Guignol, Guignol!" Poor Guignol has a good heart but he gets into trouble helping his friends or neighbors. In the show we saw he was trying to find a lost cat and the children tried to shout him advice, but Guignol's trials and tribulations continued until the last-minute happy ending. Of course I would have enjoyed it more if I had gotten to sit with the children, but we were visitors and I loved it.

~~~

I considered the works in the *Musée D'Orsay* to be the last great visual expressions of humanity's heart and soul before the near destruction of humanity itself in WWI and its aftershock WWII. Like many Americans I was in awe of the artists: Pissarro, Monet, Renoir, Cezanne, Toulouse Lautrec, Van Gogh and Gauguin. I was excited by Edgar Degas' great sculpture *Petite dan seuse de quatorze* (Little Fourteen-Year Old Dancer): an inspired peek at all the budding ballerinas in the world.

~~~

Surrounded by millennia of civilization, Nancy and I walked with two of our hand puppets to the small plaza in front of the Theatre de l'Odeon. We stood before the enlarged posters advertising William Shakespeare's play *King Lear* to be performed in French and held our hands up like North American shamans to let all the people who passed, and hopefully the children in them and us, see and watch our puppets happily sing and dance.

~~~

The train from Paris took us through the Alsacian area around Strasbourg and across the river Rhine to Munich.

I stubbornly ignored the staff woman at the information booth who reminded me of the psychologist who had wanted to send me to the Camarillo Mental Hospital when I was twenty-three. I got Nancy to ask her a long list of questions which got us directions in perfect English to a clean spacious room rented by some cordial Hindu Indian people nearby and made our way to the Marianplatz area of Old Town.

~~~

We were amazed to see the larger than life bronze statues of dairy cows on our way to the *Viktualienmarkt* (open air market).

We made it to the puppet theatre Papa Schmid and Count von Pocci founded in 1858. We saw a matinee performance of *Sleeping Beauty* with children and their parents. That evening we joined young daters, newlyweds and older married couples for an adult performance of one of Mozart's operas about young lovers getting together in Arabia.

That afternoon we toured the City's wondrous puppet collection at the Munich *Stadtmuseum* where we saw over a thousand puppets, it seemed, in various stages of completion. They even had two ¾ life-size Bunraku puppets, a male and female, in lavish costumes from Japan. I had seen pictures of most of these puppets in books in my own book collection and now got to see them eye-to-eye like long lost friends. Between all the sculptures and puppets, we had seen a vast range of human characters that, I felt, were even richer treasure than the ice cream we were still childlike enough to appreciate.

I remembered being in Campbell Hall at the University of California at Santa Barbara watching the Japanese Bunraku Theatre from Osaka, Japan. Rena and I were seated directly in front of the poet Kenneth Rexroth and his friend who were talking about when they first saw the Bunraku master puppeteers in Japan. The three-quarter life-size puppets were each animated by three puppeteers while an orchestra with Asian instruments played a traditional score and the narrator sang operatically all of the roles. The plays were about samurais who lived by their warrior bushido code of loyalty to their lords. The heroes and heroines lived, loved and died within the rigid confines of their culture. The shows were magical. They were the most awe-inspiring theatrical performances I had ever seen.

The next day I had an anxiety attack in the English Garden. When Nancy and I got in a line to order something to eat, the line wrapped around us like the walls of a maze and we became surrounded by Germans speaking German and I freaked.

What was I afraid of?

The Nazis?

I imagined I was in an apartment in Prague during World War II.

I stood up and the mattress moved. Moonlight streaked through the white embroidered curtains hanging in front of the window. Rena moved under the blankets but her eyes stayed closed. She was asleep and quiet. I stared at the blue Star of David hanging from the chain around the tendons of her neck.

I felt myself shivering but the flesh hanging from the hard bones in my legs seemed numb as I walked barefoot across the rug toward the window.

The embroidered curtains felt warm and coarse against the coldness in my hands. "Heirloom," she had told me. "They belonged to my mother, and to my grandmother. They were one of my grandmother's wedding gifts." I rubbed the double thickness of the old thread on one of the hems between my fingers and pulled her treasured curtains away from the window.

Cattle cars, I thought.

Boxcars.

"Rena, they're packing people in."

I heard the rattling, rumbling sounds of the train. The boxcars rattled. The floor and walls shook from the concussion of the iron rails of the tracks beneath. I smelled the stench of the filth buried in the damp straw on the cold planks of the floor while I felt the wood slivers of the boards puncturing the skin and bones on my hands and knees.

German SS guards aimed their machine guns at all of us who had gotten off the train. My back was stiff. Trying to stand up straight for the first time in days, I clutched the front of my frayed coat. I felt a tightening in my chest. I found it difficult to breathe.

I imagined Rena and I were running in the dark. I heard the sound of our shoes and the boots of the soldiers behind us hitting the ground. The hems of their black leather jackets swished like scythes between the front of their legs and the faster legs of their dogs. Rena stumbled and started to fall. I grabbed for her arm. I caught her wrist. I could feel my hand squeezing her skin painfully to the bone. The dogs growled behind us. I saw the look of horror behind the tears glistening in her eyes as a beam of moonlight stretched across the high cheekbones on the top half of her face. I felt her warm fingers pressing against my arm. "SS," she gasped. The soldiers raised their machine guns. The dark turned a bright black. I heard the dogs' paws pounding the pavement.

"Rena."

Clawing my fingernails into my eyelids, I stared at the darkness and slobbered on my wrists.

I thought Rena was far away and running in the middle of the night through a sewer buried under a bombed building in Warsaw. Alone underground in the dark, she looked so little and small. Lifting her arm over her shoulder, she flung herself out into the shadows of a street to throw a lit Molotov bomb.

~~~

I wasn't with Rena; I was with Nancy.

Traveling on to Salzburg, Austria, we found the famous *Salzburgher Marionettentheater* where puppeteers with extraordinary-looking string puppets perform Mozart operas to recorded music, only to be shocked because it was still closed and wouldn't open for another week. I'd goofed, but we at least got to see dozens of their earlier puppets in display windows all over town.

~~~

We celebrated May Day in non-industrial Innsbruck, the former capitol of the Tyrol at the foot of the Austrian Alps. We paid homage to the milky, frothy green glacier water in the Inn River, to the beautiful parks and gardens and the houses and shops. We ate a lot of venison sausage.

We rode the shuttle bus, the funicular and the lift up the mountain to the top of the glacier and pretended to dance and skate amid the ice-moist clouds. I rediscovered my gratitude for being alive. She smiled. I smiled. We rode halfway down the mountain laughing until we walked on to the Alpine Zoo and watched the wolves, moose and other wildlife that people like us had confined behind bars.

May every child in every being be completely healthy and happy and be able to know it and to feel it.

Peace, I thought. Por favor, bitte, s'il vous plait… please.

~~~

Now at home on European trains, Nancy and I sat back and daydreamed over our trip, our lives, and the Alps—and then the vast golden orange-yellow mustard and lively light-blue lavender fields back to Paris.

PART THREE

I looked out from around my booth and saw a young couple sitting with three kids with messed up hairdos, laughing with excitement, waiting for the puppet show to start.

Even using my microphone and built-in rechargeable battery speaker system, I let all the air out of my lungs and took my last deep breath before I started.

I slid my left hand down Wolfie's glove and brought him up off his hook and onto my index finger, little finger and thumb.

Wolfie moaned and screamed in his soft Count Dracula voice, "I'm so hungry. I haven't had a slice of pepperoni pizza in a whole month. Maybe they got a bird taco up on top of this—." He climbed left and right up the back of the proscenium arch. When he reached the peak, he fell. "M-o-u-n-t-a-i-n!" Wolfie screamed as he fell behind the booth, hit the foot of the mountain, bounced back up into the air on the one side and then twice more on the other.

"Boing! Boing! Boing!" I yelled.

Wolfie rose again, came down and crashed in the rosebush at the center of the playboard.

"Ugh," he shouted, "that hurt my snout." Then he glared at the thirty people in the audience. "Which one of you put that thorn in the rosebush?"

A couple children laughed and giggled.

"Don't you laugh at me I'm bigger than you, Shorty." Wolfie shook himself like a dog does when it's all wet. "Okay, you gonna let me eat your little toe for a snack? Or what? Come on, you got two."

"Duh, duh!" Red said.

"Ah, ha!" Wolfie shouted. "I'm going to hide in the bushes. Now nobody can see me."

Wolfie hid in the bushes and raised his left paw high over his head.

"I see you," a kid said.

"No, you don't," Wolfie said. "Don't argue with me, Kid. I'm a grown-up. I know what I'm talking about."

"No, you don't."

"Duh, duh!" Red Riding Hood sang, belting it out, as she entered on the audience's left side of the stage. She bowed. "Usually I get a little applause when I make my entrance. I'm a child actress on the stage of life." She bowed again. The audience applauded her.

"Hey!" Wolfie exclaimed as he jumped out of the bushes and pointed at Red. "That's kid meat on a stick. That's a kid-ka-bob. That's going over my barbecue pit."

Wolfie cleared his throat.

"Hello, Darling," he said, bowing.

Red turned to the audience and said, "Doesn't he sound like a wonderful gentleman?"

"No, he's not a gentleman. He's a wolf," one kid shouted.

Wolfie looked around behind Red Riding Hood. Then he asked, "What're you doing all alone in the woods?"

"I'm going to Grandma's house," she said. "My Grandma's big. She's wonderful."

Wolfie drooled and slurped it off his lips. "So glad to hear that. Where does your wonderful Grandma live?"

"My Grandma lives in Grandma's house. Down the path behind the tree and the big rock."

Wolfie looked at Red, looked at the audience and then looked back at Red.

"That's pretty close to my front teeth," he said. Then he looked toward the audience. "If Grandma's bigger than the little kid, I'll eat Grandma for breakfast. And then I'll eat the kid for dessert."

"Whaa, whaa!" Red started crying.

"What's the matter?" Wolfie asked.

"Whaa, whaa!" Red cried again. "My Grandma looks awful. She's got a bad cold all over her whole face. And my little brother said Grandma looks like a rubber chicken."

"That's great!" Wolfie said, and laughed.

A few people out in the audience shook their heads.

"No, it's not," one kid shouted.

"A sick Grandma will be a whole lot easier for me to catch." Then to Red he said, "Kid, if you take these beautiful flowers to your wonderful Grandma it'll make her look and feel a whole lot better."

"Really, Mr. Wolfie? Really?" Red grabbed him by the snout so hard she knocked him to the ground underneath her. Rising slowly, she got up and backed off.

Wolfie got up and looked her right in the eyes.

"Would I tell you a lie?"

Wolfie and Red both looked out at the audience and held their pose in silence.

"Don't answer that," Wolfie screamed at the audience.

"Well, if it works, I'll try it," Red said. "I love my Grandma."

"How sweet," Wolfie said.

"I'll go up the hill and get flowers for my Grandma."

"Get her a whole bunch."

Red exited stage right.

Wolfie howled. "Everybody howl," he told the audience. And the audience did, "Au-woo!" And then Wolfie exited under the playboard.

Red entered and strolled around the stage, singing:

> "Hills and hills of lovely flowers.
> She likes the yellows and the red ones.
> These are nice and these are nicer.
> I'm getting flowers for my Grandma."

"Let me out!" Grandma shouted. "I'm a Lady-type person and I don't belong in a blue pillow case." Red has exited the stage.

"Nope," Wolfie said, coming up and going down, entering and exiting, with a stuffed blue bag in his arms. He's now wearing rimless glasses and a white wig.

"I'm a senior citizen," Grandma shouted.

"Nope," Wolfie repeated.

"You let me out of this bag, or I'm gonna…"

"No violence, Grandma." Wolfie dropped the blue bag on the playboard. "I'm bigger and smarter than Grandma. And I'm better looking."

"Knock, knock. Grandma, it's me the kid. The door's stuck. Let me in," Red Riding Hood shouted from the top of the booth.

"Ah, ha!" Wolfie said. "I'm gonna change my voice and make her think I'm her Grandmother and get her into the house." He coughed a couple times to clear his throat.

"Come on in to Grandma's little house," he said using the least terrible of his Grandma voices. And in his worst wolf voice he added, "Get in here, Kid."

"That didn't sound like a grandma," someone said.

"Yes, it did," Wolfie said. "It sounded just like your grandmother."

"You're C-R-A-Z-Y!" a kid screamed.

Red Riding Hood entered, holding a lot of flowers.

"It's the Wolf! It's the Wolf!" a kid screamed.

"Oh, I hope the flowers look good. I love my Grandma so much, but I never saw her sick before and it scares me."

"Come to Grandma, Dear. I miss you so much," Wolfie said. "Ha, ha. I know it's not fair. She's just a little kid. But I'm hungry. It's not my fault I'm a genius."

"It's the Wolf!" someone shouted.

"I'm coming, Grandma. Hey, Everybody, check this out. This is gonna be fun to play with." Red shouted, starting to pull on Wolfie's ears.

Wolfie screamed.

People laughed.

"You stop laughing. It hurts."

"My Grandma's got two new fluffy ears for me to play with."

"Ouch!" Wolfie shouted. "She nearly pulled my ears out of my head. She can't do this to me. She's a little girl."

"Grandma, what big eyes you have," Red said, starting to shake Wolfie's head and slapping his temples with her hands. "Why? Why? Why?" she demanded, constantly changing the tone of her voice. "Why, Grandma? Why? Everybody, ask Grandma why?"

People asked, "Why?"

"Grandma, you've got some really sharp, nasty, dirty-looking teeth on this side of your snout. Grandma, you've got more sharp, dirty teeth on this side of your..." Then she asked the audience, "Does my Grandma got a snout?"

"He's not your Grandma. He's the Wolf!" one boy screamed.

"Grandma, why you got sharp teeth?"

"The better to eat you with, Kid." Wolfie said in his own voice.

"You're not my grandma."

"No way, Honey."

"Help, help!" Red screamed as she exited down right.

"That proves I'm smarter than all the grandmas and kids in the whole world put together, right?"

"No!" the audience screamed.

"Now, I'm gonna run over there and eat my breakfast. Au-woo!" Wolfie crashed into the black backdrop.

Some kids and their parents started laughing loud.

"Don't laugh. I can't see."

I stepped out from behind the booth.

"Folks," I said. "I'm not going to let this poor misguided wolf starve to death. So, I'm going to give him a hamburger so people can laugh at him tomorrow. Okay? But, Ladies, he's been naughty, rude and obnoxious in public so I'm going to put the hottest mustard we've got in town all over it. Kids, don't tell him about the hot mustard. It's our little secret. Okay?"

"Where's the kid?" Wolfie asked. "There she is, there she is!"

Red re-entered with a rubber hamburger.

"We'd like to give you this hot mustard. Uh, I mean hamburger. So you don't get sick and yuck." she said, falling down, pretending to be throwing up and dying.

75

"You nice people want me to eat this hamburger so I don't yuck?"

"It's all for you, Wolfie," Red said.

"Really? I love it. Everybody yell, 'Eat it, Wolfie,' and I'll do it."

"1-2-3…" Wolfie counted.

"Eat it, Wolfie!" the audience screamed.

"Au-woo!" Wolfie howled as he lunged for the burger. "Oh, yum."

"He likes it," Red said.

"Before I get another hamburger from the Puppet Man, everybody howl like a wolf on a hot summer night. Au-woo!" Wolfie howled.

"Before I get my precious Grandma out of the bag, everybody, clap your hands and yell, 'Yea, Grandma!'" Red shouted.

"Yeah, Grandma!" the audience screamed.

"I love you, Grandma." she said.

And Grandma said, "I love you, too, dear."

I slid Wolfie and Red Riding Hood off my hands and returned them to hang upside down from their hooks on the outer edge of the propboard and I stepped out from behind the booth to face the audience.

"Thank you for helping my little girl not be eaten for Wolfie's breakfast," I said. "Everybody raise your hands. Touch your heart. Every one of us has a child inside us, and some of us have a small child beside us. And we want all our children to be healthy. Clap your hands, please."

The seventy-plus people now in the audience clapped their hands.

"A little faster, now," I said. "That's it."

~~~

I was winded from coming up the stairs but breathing. The wound through my ribs stung whenever I turned and stretched my upper body left or right, or up and down, like I had just done walking up the single flight of stairs.

I ducked my head under the German doll holding the brown caterpillar fur club in his fist hanging from the yellow planter hook in the ceiling. I sat the Pharmacy bag with my minor painkillers in it on the metal table, passed my heavy performance schedule calendar on the refrigerator and moved toward the faucet over the sink and poured myself a glass of water.

76

Last week I walked to this open kitchen window. I was trying to breathe, but I couldn't. So I turned back and sat down in a chair directly in front of a small electric fan on the table. I turned it on to force air into my lungs. It helped, and I didn't panic, but I still felt like I couldn't breathe. Three minutes later, I stood up and walked to the door and opened it to call out for help if anyone was home, if my voice still worked, if anyone heard me, while my blood pressure rose enough to lift me up into a heart attack or a stroke.

Nancy met me out in the hall. She helped me decide to call 911. She followed the ambulance that rushed me to the Emergency Room at French Hospital. She called my brothers.

Strange to be back, I thought.

I had lived to be fifty-eight years old.

My generation thought we would all die by the age of thirty. I had thought about that while I watched the saline solution entering my body through the IV and the air, blood and other liquids leaving my chest through the tube connected to the pump on the floor beside my bed. The doctors were emptying the cavity that had expanded around my collapsed right lung to reduce it to make room for my lung to re-inflate as much as possible.

Eventually thinking I might not be joking about the tube and the wound in my chest not hurting, the surgeon on duty said it should be, so on the third day he pulled the tube out of my lung and ribs and jabbed it back in and I went through the roof of a sideshow of horror.

~~~

My wound stung when I stretched the skin and flesh.

I tried to breathe one breath at a time and appreciate it because my lungs could collapse again. And it could be worse.

~~~

Back home now and wondering how long I might have left to live, I reached for my wooden blond Little Boy puppet with my left hand and ran my right hand up into the glove under his costume, my index finger into his hollow neck and my thumb and pinky into his cloth arms all the way out to his hand carved basswood hands.

"You're back!" my naturally cheerful little kid shouted.

"Well," I said. "Give us a hug, Luv."

Little Boy leaned his chest against my mouth, placed the side of his head between my cheek and my nose and pressed his cloth arms and wooden hands around my chin.

"There, there," I said. "Did you miss me?"

"No," he snapped.

"No?" I said. "So, why didn't you finish making and painting these props I left here?"

Little Boy looked me in the face, glanced down at the unfinished props on the table and then looked back into my eyes.

No answer.

"You have been rehearsing, right?"

"Nope," he said. "Puppet Man, you know I don't do stuff when you're not here."

"You don't? Why not?"

"I watch cartoons. I'm a kid."

"A kid," I said. "I thought you were my grandfather."

"No, you didn't."

"Yes, I did. He's a short little old man just like you are."

Little Boy made a sound at the back of his mouth and laughed.

"No, I'm not." he said. "You're silly."

"Yes, I am," I said, and then I hugged him with my shoulder and my other hand.

~~~

I saw the sunlight and the shadows on the opposite sides of everything I looked at. Everything seemed to have a moveable glaze of something more transparent than plexiglass encapsulating it.

Everything still comes back to the light, I thought, and to the mind.

I could sense things but I felt like my head was out of whack. I was off-balance. And dizzy.

I took long walks, watched what I ate, rested and eventually got some strength back. I stopped and looked at people and buildings, at birds and trees and at mountains and creeks and at the skies. I mused on things endlessly. I often took strolls without a destination and sat on curbs, benches and short ledges and thought about all kinds of things. I also looked at my unpolished poems and worked on them a little two or three times a day.

I was still too sore to laugh. Laughing even a little hurt.

~~~

Two weeks after I was released, my surgeon Dr. Hayashi said, "Your lung's back to 95% and the wound's healing fine. I want you to start getting rigorous exercise, aggressive workouts, stop and take a walk after every hour of physical inactivity. You'll work better with blood and oxygen getting to your brain. Do all the puppet shows you want… and go climb mountains."

"I'm fine?"

"Yes. Aggressive exercise. Lots of it."

Driving home feeling confused and yet lighthearted, I remembered Milo and I bouncing on hay piles and how the pieces of dry hay slid up under our shirts, itched and tickled us in the heat on the farms in our childhood.

~~~

How about I see a lot more young dads holding their small children way up in the air on their shoulders, the children holding their daddies' foreheads with their palms and in their arms and men and women, both, sitting on the pavement in the street beside their kids and sometimes holding one or two of their children in their laps?

~~~

"Ring!"

The land phone rang.

"Ring!"

"Ring!"

I picked up.

An older man asked, "Is this Donald Wallis?"

"Yes," I said. "I'm Don."

"Mr. Wallis, I'm Dr.—, the coroner of Santa Clara County. You're the brother of Milo Wallis who resides at… in San Jose, California?"

"Coroner?" I asked myself. And in that instant something more primal and familiar in my head than I had ever realized changed forever.

"Yes," I said. I paused. I added: "Sir, you're phoning me to tell me my brother's dead?"

I squeezed the phone receiver like I was a starving eagle clawing the throat of a small rabbit.

"Your brother was found early this morning at his home. Our initial examination concluded that he died late last night from a possible heart attack."

"Did he suffer long, Sir?"

I felt myself clenching my jaw and grinding my teeth and pushing my guts back into my abdomen with my fingers.

"There were no signs of prolonged trauma. It appeared that he died quickly, even possibly in his sleep."

"Good," I said. "Thank you, Sir."

"He has another brother, John Wallis, residing in Fresno? Is that correct?"

"Our youngest brother, John. Yes. I was the oldest."

"Yes, Mr. Wallis. I must phone John next. And I'll do that right now, Sir. If you have any questions later, you can phone me at… "

I repeated the number back to him as I wrote it down, slowly.

"That's correct. I am sorry for your loss, Mr. Wallis."

"Thank you. May the rest of your day go well, Sir," I said.

There was a short pause.

"Good-bye," he said.

I waited seven or eight minutes before I phoned John. We talked for maybe ten minutes through our tears. And then we hung up.

~~~

Be clear and practical.

Calendar. Checkbook. Money. Travel bag. Map. Address. Phone numbers. Messages. Call. Car. Water. Air. Gas. Oil.

Checking.

Cash in my Kerr glass jar bank. Recounted three times before I put it into my wallet, check. Heavy-duty black over-the-shoulder airline bag packed for two nights. Three nights, check. Messages for Nancy, Ken, Marvin and Einar, check. "Milo's died. I'm going to John's to be with my family. Sunday, I'll be back. No problem. Don't worry." Check. Pain medicine, fresh bandages, check. Drink at least a third of a glass of water. Feelings went, like gas into my gas tank, into my stomach. Check, check, check.

80

Milo, I'm sorry. I hope you're all right.

What am I saying?

Don, you alienated, isolated human being.

Drive, Man. Just drive.

~~~

I remembered nearly blinding Milo when I shot a homemade arrow into the sky and he stood there looking at it until it hit him between his nose and his right eye. I was eleven; Milo was nine.

I remembered my dad being knifed in the side of his lower abdomen by a drunken visitor in our home late one night. I was seven; Milo was five.

~~~

"We would have come to see you in the hospital, but..."

"No, I told you not to, John. I was fine. Your kids are all working and Milo wanted to see his first grandchild, and did. That was important. That was real important."

"Yeah. He got to see her," my kid brother repeated. "Right."

"Milo sounded real happy on the phone the last I talked with him, John. He was actually giggling."

John nodded.

My sister-in-law Denise caught my attention and kept it.

John turned around and walked away to get something. I tried to keep my eye on the back of his camouflaged khaki shirt but it faded as he walked away.

My youngest brother Sergeant John Wallis trained Air Force police to protect and defend people, bombers, jets and munitions. He had just made it home safe after being stationed for six months in one of our U.S. air bases high in the central mountains of Asia in Kyrgyzstan west of China, north of Afghanistan and east of Iraq (and Iran).

Denise stepped closer and looked up in my face.

"We all talked it over and we would like you to speak at the service, Don, to say something about Milo for everyone. Will you?"

"Sure, Denise. I'll write it out. Something short."

I nodded.

John returned. Denise walked away into the next room and then upstairs to give us a chance to be alone together.

"Here, Don," John said. He handed me a red banner with a gold-colored hammer and sickle and braided trim. "I got this for you just before I came home from Kyrgyzstan. It's the former Soviet flag."

"You got me a communist flag?"

"I thought you'd like it."

"I do. I'm just surprised you…"

"I got teased but only by a couple guys. A guy was selling a lot of these," John said. "I thought I'd wait until I saw you to give it to you."

"I'm glad you're home," I said.

"Yeah," he said.

"We're here but Milo…" I put my hand on John's chest and patted him on his heart. "They're all gone. Dad. Mom. Now Milo."

We had hugged each other and cried together already but we weren't done. Our throats and our lips were trembling. Our eyes were still wet. We fumbled our words like backfield football players fumbling the ball playing in the rain or like we were moving our lips like they were our legs and feet and we were stumbling in mud.

"I respect you, John. And I'm proud of you," I said. And then I blurted out, "You just damn well make sure you don't die before I do. You hear me?"

My huge 6'3" kid brother, the Air Force sergeant who could protect a briefcase or a Stealth bomber single-handed if he had to, looked downward into my eyes and then he snapped like a severely weakened steel beam and collapsed in my arms, crying, his body quaking, sobbing his grief out of his lungs, shaking the house and us.

"I love you, Brother. It's all right, John. Let it out."

~~~

I remembered once upon a time when Milo and I walked long narrow dirt roads between pastures, olive groves and strawberry fields outside Stockton and Manteca, side-by-side, our legs and feet in partnered unison, brushing the knuckles on our fingers, the bones on our wrists, our elbows, our knees and ankles. And when we ran through fire and ashes, chasing Dad as he dragged a burning jumbo tractor tire on foot to clear a melon field of weeds north of Modesto, 90 miles west of Yosemite. And when we splashed our feet and toes in the Pacific

Ocean, clamming with Dad at Pismo Beach, the small salty waves rising to our knees, to our waists, to our chests. Or later, much later, when Mom, Dad, Milo and I sprinted to little three year-old John who sat in the sandy dirt at Nacimiento Lake between Monterey and San Luis Obispo counties, crying, with dozens of large red ants crawling between the folds of his baby-pink scrotum and Mom and Dad kept pulling them off him and John kept crying until our whole family saved him from the vicious mandibles of the ants.

~~~

I worked on writing out something appropriate to say about Milo to the family and his friends at the service. See it, feel it and maybe even act it out, I thought. Just jot down whatever words first come to mind and then add more on sheet after sheet of yellow legal pad paper. Build sentences. Then paragraphs. Rearrange the parts to make the phrases sound more natural, rhythmical and to make more sense, to be clearer by finally tightening and condensing, editing, cutting out every unnecessary word, sentence and paragraph, sculpting, modeling and carving and polishing, smoothing it all out after many passes.

Trust the process.

I thought about asking some of my friends to go with me to the service so I could have them there for their support, as Marvin would say. I decided to ask Nancy, Marvin, Einar, my young friend Derek Niles and Bob Liepman. Ken had been to enough funerals.

My friends had been close to me for five to thirty years. I wanted them near me to remind me who and where I was so I could do what I had to do.

~~~

"No, Milo. No, John. No, don't come down," I had told my two younger brothers on the phone from the hospital. "I'm fine. I'm gonna be okay. Besides, Milo, you're going to see your first grandchild. Go. You're finally a grandfather, Milo. Don't come down here."

I felt hollow in my stomach, in my chest and in my head. I thought I was a fool losing people.

With the start of fresh tears in the corners of my eyes, I remembered reading about the Russian writer Leo Tolstoy dying at a train depot in rural Russia. Tolstoy was now asleep forever. An internationally known author, a man who had lived his life so wide-awake and who had communicated with so many people and yet, at the end, no one knew what was really going on in his mind. And maybe he didn't either.

~~~

I had my typed speech folded and shoved into my long sleeve Bordeaux cherry shirt pocket. My old brown leather belt held up my black slacks and the cuffs of my slacks concealed my workingman's white cotton socks and my brown leather shoes.

Nancy drove me to the Madonna Inn. Milo's daughter Melissa had rented the Wine Cellar Room down in the basement.

Marvin and Derek joined Nancy and I at one of the large round tables. So did my friend Bob Liepman with his cello. They sat together while I got back up and greeted more people who were arriving. I hugged and shook hands with relatives, former relatives-in-law and people Milo had worked with: a total of a hundred people altogether. We all were sad and formal. Some of us were tearful in the eyes, and some of us were drowning in the throat.

I sat down.

I kept thinking I had outlived Milo. The filled room looked empty without him. I tried not to look at his picture on the display easel near the podium.

I was very apprehensive about the speech. I drummed my hands and tapped my fingers on my thighs and up on top of the table.

"I'm really nervous about this, you guys," I said to my friends. "Nancy, I'm so glad I went to visit him last fall in San Francisco. I'm so glad I did that. I can see and hear him laughing, and then that serious exhausted look on his face."

"Everyone in this room's on your side," Marvin said.

Bob nodded.

"That's right," Derek said.

"It's not a performance," Nancy said. "You can just read it."

"I can?"

"Yes."

Melissa went to the podium. She welcomed everyone briefly and said a few things about her father.

"And now Uncle Don will speak to us," she said, looking toward me for something inside me, from me, I didn't think I had.

It went through my mind that I knew Milo when we were children, a little, and not much since. Then I thought that I did know my brother real well, but not anyone in the room now at all.

Dad, Mom, Milo...

Only John and I were left.

And I knew I had to get up and do it.

So I did.

~~~

"Welcome, Everybody," I said. "Thank you for coming to Milo's memorial. We all shared his energy, his friendship and his work.

"My brother Milo was the first friend I ever had. We shared the blood in our hearts and the air in our lungs. We were inseparable for the first ten years of his life. We clutched our two Panda Bears and each other in the corner in the dark and under our beds, frightened of the lightning and thunderstorms in the San Joaquin Valley.

"Milo was born on March 5, 1948, in Napa, California. He died 56 years old. Our parents named Milo after our dad's father Milo Wilsie Wallis.

"Mom grew up on a farm in Wasco, California. Milo and I watched her stay up all night on the small twenty-acre farm we had in Manteca making sick baby calves swallow raw egg yolks to keep them alive. We also watched her put cold washcloths on our foreheads when we had the fever and work sixteen hours a day to keep us alive.

"Dad rode the rails from Ohio to Washington State to California for three years during the Depression. He started when he was eleven years old. 6'4", he served in the Army Communication Corps and followed General Douglas MacArthur through Borneo, New Guinea and the Philippines and into Japan.

"Milo was devastated when he was eleven because he thought our dad had deserted him. Milo found a heavy blanket of bravado and

85

started wearing it over his head to protect himself from being hurt again. That's what made him, as our sister Denise says, look like a grizzly bear instead of the teddy bear that's inside him. It took my brave brother four decades to overcome that sorrow, and he mellowed, finding more of the truth and more love and compassion.

"Milo could say no. He could sound gruff and even snarl showing the teeth on the side of his mouth like a protective growling dog.

"Milo was incapable of deserting anyone he loved or cared about.

"Milo could feel.

"He loved Tammy when they found each other. They married and he enjoyed being a member of her family.

"He worked. Truck drivers haul a lot of food, medicine and other things that families all over the country need to live, he told me, and he did the best he could to keep their trucks on the road. He ordered the parts the mechanics needed. He was proud to do it. And he loved and was loyal to that family, too.

"Milo remained close to our younger brother Johnny Lee Wallis and his wife Denise and their three children: Mona, Kelly and Robert, while his own child Melissa grew up getting to talk to her dad about anything she thought or felt. He got to see Melissa happily married to a fine young man named Dale Dasker. And then he got to see and hold his lovely granddaughter, their beautiful baby, Alexandra Rose.

"His older brother... I am grateful for that.

"Milo would repeat himself endlessly."

Several people laughed. Then many joined in.

"Sometimes I think it's a family trait. He used to say everything he said to me at least three times. To make sure I knew I had my facts right, and/or that my conclusion was correct. To let me know he cared. That he agreed. Milo was a reflective human being as his daughter Melissa realized. He listened. He heard us. He supported and defended us. He joined us and he strengthened us. He even went with me to San Francisco twice and walked all over the place. The last time was a year ago and then he told me he didn't think he could do it again. Until now I did not fully know what he might have meant.

"Milo was a person I will continue to incorporate into my life for as long as I live. Milo was a blessing. Milo was Milo. And I'm glad I knew him.

"Before we are silent for a few moments while my friend Bob Liepman plays a piece by Bach on his cello for us to honor my brother, and before we watch the computerized still-photo movie of Milo's life with us that our family has made to go with the soundtrack of Creedence Clearwater Revival's *Put A Candle In The Window* and Waylon Jenning's *My Heroes Have Always Been Cowboys* would everyone, first, please rise. Please stand. Would everyone in this room, everyone in the world, please join me in giving my brother Milo Wallis a standing ovation for having lived his full and beautiful life, which he did so well."

And we all applauded loud and long.

"Thank you."

~~~

Normally I would have worked on a poem immediately after losing someone. Especially Milo, I thought. But now I wanted to see him. I wanted to get as close to him as I could. So with my dad on my left shoulder and my mom on my right and Milo on my head looking down over my forehead, I shut my door and actually locked it. I drew Milo in pencil. I transferred the drawing to a canvas. I stood in front of my easel and redrew only the necessary lines and shadows. Then I started the long process of painting, a grisaille, the values of darks, mid-tones and lights until I got them all correct and I felt like the piece was a true representation of the real him.

I looked intensely at the sorrowful shadows in the corners of my own eyes. I remembered crying so many times before. I felt so dehydrated and hollow again.

I worked on Milo's portrait in the late mornings and early afternoons. I put thin glazes of a few mixed colors over the black and white under-painting. I stared at things that I knew he had had inside him, things I knew he had thought about and felt. I stared into my memories of his eyes, his mouth, his nose, and his hands.

I worked until my fingers trembled like my eyelashes and struck each other like logs being washed down the river of my eyes melting into the white froth of the saltwater on the soaked and bruised edges of my eyelids.

I thought about mute people using sign language rapidly because they had so much they wanted to talk about as I wiped my eyes dry with my fingers.

~~~

"You're not alone and you're not sick, Don. Not now. You've got your family and you've got good friends," Nancy said. "I'm usually calm, you're a whole Broadway cast."

"Thanks," I said.

"You're welcome," she said.

"Enough," I said.

~~~

I thought about Milo.

I don't remember us ever really fighting until he was ten. I felt him kick me in the shins a few times and I watched him frown and turn away and run off to Dad. When Milo and I were men I smelled the smoke from charcoal brickets and the grease from barbecued sausages… and the same smell of burning cigarettes and green-stinging beer on him I had smelled on my dad. Work hard. Act tough. Inhale carcinogens. Eat fat. Die from it.

I saw Milo grinning with his chipped tooth below his dark-haired mustache.

I had memories of him still inside me, memories of when he was a little boy… and plenty of feelings. Pee Wee, we called him. And I needed to go off by myself to figure out what I thought.

~~~

I retreated to a familiar place up the coast at Big Sur. I camped near a stream and some redwoods.

The third day, I spent the afternoon working on some old poems without any interruptions. Solitude and being out in Nature changed my perspective, and my intention. And the final rewrites seemed more honest.

That evening, just before sunset, I watched seagulls flying back toward the ocean through the shadows between the trees. I reached for a solid-looking stick I had sat near my feet and pushed the start of burning coals under the fresh logs on my campfire.

I was soon alone in the dark except for the stars and the moon, and the heat from the fire. I pushed more hot coals in closer toward a log that had started to burn. Three deer passed within thirty feet and a coyote got within six feet of me before he realized it because I was very quiet and covered with smoke.

Listening to ocean waves crashing against the cliffs, rocks and sand nearby, I thought about how old I had become. I thought about my life, and how I felt about the way I had lived it. I thought about how I still didn't know much. I thought about my friends. I thought about cleaning my greasy fingers tomorrow, or the next day, and putting my clean hands back into two of my puppets.

Hearing a train from somewhere way deep in the back of my mind, I looked up and thought for a moment I might see an old freight train crossing the sky. I thought about my dad being a hobo. I thought about my brothers smiling while we hugged each other again just last summer.

~~~

Before I went back to do my next scheduled shows at the Nipomo Swap Meet, I looked again at the 1905 photograph of Papa Schmid sitting with his arms folded looking at his marionette Kasper who stands facing him on a hand carved square-top wooden table in Munich. A little boy with short hair stands barefoot on a stool with his forearms folded across his small chest, leaning on the table. The dimple-cheeked little boy smiles, staring at Kasper's big red cheeks and Papa Schmid's angelic-looking face. Kasper is talking to Papa Schmid, and is obviously saying something funny. The old man and the very young little boy look quite amused. They both are grinning.

~~~

"You back?" ten year-old Medardo at the Nipomo Swap Meet asked. "You hunting Koala Bears in Africa?"

"Australia, I think."

"Australia," he repeated and laughed. "Right."

I rubbed the thick black hair on the top of his head. Then I took my hat off and let him rub my baldhead with both of his hands.

"It's good to see you," I said. "I want you to remember I told you: you are a good person, a fine young boy and you are my friend, and I'm very glad that I know you. Please remember that. Okay?"

"You gonna fire me?"

"No, you little goof. I love you, Kid."

We walked over to the ladies in the small Mexican cafe and I bought us our usual burrito carne assada with homemade salsa, red sauce and everything which included white onions, cilantro, rice, beans, chopped steak, cheese and lime, and we split it.

Medardo set up most of my booth by himself and said he would stay and watch the new show but not the old ones. He was a busy kid.

~~~

The Naughty Naughty entered the stage slowly.

Little Boy leaned over the top of the booth and waved at the audience.

"If you guys see the Kid," the Naughty Naughty said. "Tell him to wait right here because I'm gonna put him in the Yuckie Bucket and stir it with a stick and squish him like a little green bug."

Medardo said, "Yeah, right."

Another kid laughed.

"Okay?" the Naughty Naughty said and exited.

Little Boy entered the stage. He coughed, using his hand to cover his mouth. He sang,

> "Me, me, me.
> My big brother said,
> me look like a little monkey
> and—my mom and daddy
> gonna put me in the zoo.
> Yea!"

Little Boy clapped his hands and bowed. "Thank you," he said.

The Naughty Naughty entered and shouted, "He's gonna get it."

Little Boy ducked under the playboard.

The Naughty Naughty leaned down over the playboard. "Is the Kid down there?" he asked. "No." He rose and moved to the opposite side of the stage. "Is he down there? No," he said. Then he ran to the far side of the booth where he screamed in his high shrill voice as if he was falling thousands of feet. "He's right down—there!"

Little Boy popped over the top of the booth and yelled at the falling Naughty Naughty, "Maybe another five miles down the road!"

Little Boy ducked down.

The Naughty Naughty rose, looked up and asked, "Who said that up there?" No answer. He looked away.

Little Boy rose, shook his head and shouted, "I really shouldn't say!" Then he ducked back down.

The Naughty Naughty looked up and then away again.

Little Boy rose. "Come to think of it, maybe it was a bird," he said, and ducked.

The Naughty Naughty glared at the audience.

Little Boy rose and said, "I think it was a seagull from Pismo Beach." Then he ducked.

The Naughty Naughty looked up, saw no one and glared again at the audience.

Little Boy rose. "A big one!" he yelled. "Hey, Mister, you better get a big hat or that bird is going to poop on your head."

Little Boy ducked again.

The Naughty Naughty looked up.

The audience laughed.

"What's so funny?" the Naughty Naughty said.

Medardo was busting a gut, bending over and giggling. He looked happy.

The Naughty Naughty left the stage.

Little Boy entered.

"Great, Guys," Little Boy shouted, and applauded the audience. "Great job, Guys."

The Naughty Naughty entered from behind Little Boy and grabbed him. "Got you," he shouted.

"Let me go," Little Boy screamed. "You let me go!"

"I'm gonna put you in the bucket," the Naughty Naughty said.

Little Boy slipped free and hid behind the Naughty Naughty's back.

The Naughty Naughty faced the audience. "Where's the Kid?"

Little Boy climbed the Naughty Naughty's back. From over Naughty Naughty's head, Little Boy said, "I'm right behind you, Turkey."

Little Boy pounded on the Naughty Naughty's head with his fists. The Naughty Naughty turned around again.

"No, he's not," the Naughty Naughty said.

Again from over the back of the Naughty Naughty's head Little Boy pounded on him with his fists and shouted, "I'm still behind you, Turkey Buzzard!" Then he exited, went up and leaned over the top of the booth. "Tell him, I'm in the Yuckie Bucket," he told the audience.

"Where's the Kid?" the Naughty Naughty shouted.

"He's in the Yuckie Bucket," Medardo said.

"Yeah," Little Boy shouted. "He's probably down at the bottom!" People laughed.

"Wait 'till I get my hands on him," the Naughty Naughty said, approaching the bucket. "I'll squish him like a little green bug. Then all the kids in the world are going into the bucket. What are they good for? Nothing." The Naughty Naughty entered the bucket. He squirmed around, shouting, "Oh… ugh, my nose. This is yuckie. This is gross. This stinks."

Little Boy reentered the stage.

"Should I push him down into the bucket?" he asked the audience. "Everybody, say one-two-three together real loud, and I'll do it."

"One-two-three!"

Little Boy shoved the screaming Naughty Naughty down into the bucket.

The Naughty Naughty's hand rose and sank a total of three times.

Little Boy stirred the bucket with the stick and said, "Yes, sir. Squished like a little green bug. Clap your hands, Everybody."

The audience clapped their hands, whistled and howled.

"We're all big kids now," Little Boy said.

He bowed and exited the stage.

~~~

Medardo laughed.

"So long, Puppet Man," he said.

92

Watching him grinning as he walked away, I smiled and thought about performing my puppet shows live to all the families in the world.

~~~~~~~~~

UNTIL I GET UP ONE MORNING
AND FEEL LIKE DOING SOMETHING
Prose Poems

HOME MOVIES

I'm carrying my camera like a cross over my shoulder to protect my lenses and film because I'm worried about trip wires, bamboo traps and mortars... The camera's getting heavier like my legs. I slip and fall three times, one after the other. I'm hobbling through the slush of a rice paddy, shooting, letting the film keep eating the action.

I see my German-American grandfather and his newspaper spread out across the dinner table and my grandmother's hard-crusted bread, still hot from the oven, melting the butter on a plate she had put in front of him. I think about how she's packed him snuggly into their home and held him with the soft flesh around her arms. But I see him wadding the pages of his newspaper up like used bandages. I see blood drowning the print.

I see vegetable roots and leaves woven and wedged into the huts that still hold the farmers of this village together. This Southeast Asian country... These people who look more like thin goats than European-American men, women and children. I see the dog fleas in the cold pot of rice overturned on the ground.

I see my cousins, drinking Cokes and eating hot dogs tonight, watching the dropped napalm exploding into flames in the lead story of the evening news on television. I feel my own coolness surrounding the burning and the stench; and I feel the air digging into my lungs and the blood planting its poison in my heart.

THE TRIP

I look like I'm stepping right out of the Bible. The long hair, the sandals…

I clutch my ticket, drag my duffle bag between my knees and cross among the lepers and beggars in the San Francisco bus station. I board the northbound coach. Grab a seat. And sweating lightly, I try to get comfortable for the more than 24-hour trip to Portland… to Seattle… to Vancouver.

Knowing I may live in exile forever, I feel the warm breath of U.S. Marines at the back of my neck as I steal a soldier from the Pentagon by smuggling myself out of the most powerful nation on earth. And by the dawn's warm light, exhausted from worry, I leave my unfolded map of Washington on my empty seat and, headed for the Olympic Rainforest, I crawl out through a crack in the window.

I spread my limbs, my wings. I fly like Icarus out of prison toward the sun away from his dad. And sweating heavily, I rise on the steam rising from the dead and dying in WWI, WWII, Korea and Vietnam. The wax melts. My feathers separate and fall. And I collapse.

THE TALK WITH MY MOTHER

There are sane people in crazy houses.

No, Mom. I remember slouching the way I used to when I was sitting in my desk and something slipped and it dropped. It did. And now I can't find it. Maybe it fell under the table... but that's not funny now, now is it? Not when we're both down here on our knees. See? You look just like the Mother of God in the Vatican. It's Michelangelo's statue. The Pieta... a woman holding her son. I'm ten years younger than Jesus, Mom. I'm twenty-three. I remember I could read. Even long sentences. And I read my poems to you because you taught me my alphabet, Mom. I remember feeling I didn't want to cry all day and night. And I played outside all the time while you made me sandwiches. I used to play so deep inside my mind, so quietly all over, like I was a soap bubble hot ballooning over the grasses in the pasture searching for happiness and the weeds that still needed to be picked from the garden. I used to read about generals and emperors: Hannibal, Caesar and Napoleon. And I read about Anne Frank being unable to escape the German gas chambers and Alexander Solzhenitsyn and other dissidents in Siberia who never made it out of the Soviet prison camps: spies, scientists and poets. I remember feeling like someone needed me to do something about all of our problems but I was afraid. I need to become brave, or a coward. And I think the doctors and therapists here are gonna want me to forget about becoming a revolutionary: and join the System. But... The doctors? No, that guy holding the broom outside's not a doctor, Mom. He's an orderly. He cut my hair real short after he pretended to like me. I stood here and I watched all my long brown hair fall into little piles on the floor like the people's hair did against the pavement on campus at Berkeley... and he was laughing... like the Guardsman who aimed his loaded rifle at me (who wasn't laughing) from the corner across the street below my kitchen window. Martial law. It happened. There were pictures in The San Francisco Chronicle, Mom. Students gassed, chased and clubbed by young

Guardsmen too unfamiliar with the classics to be critical enough of their own government and by police officers with only high school educations and harsh orders to protect their country from traitors... What's happening to me's not all that uncommon. It's natural, Mom. I'm normal. I'm still normal. Even Ronald Reagan, the Governor, could wind up rubbing his hands over and over again like Pontius Pilate in trouble and dozing off in a trance like the guy mumbling verses from Cicero and The King James Version of the Bible standing over there in the corner. But I'm not... What was I saying, Mom? I forget.

AROMATHERAPY

Dennis, I inhaled smoke all last night again. I'm afraid even your asylum won't shield me from the looks on the faces of the children burning in the oil on the water.

Still warm and wet from the shower, I smelled so much soap when I entered the kitchen this morning I had difficulty lighting the burner to boil the water for coffee. I almost fell. I nearly dropped my cup.

I saw water drops on the back of my hands and on the leaves of the lush-green plants out the window.

I still heard babies' cries and mothers' screams and men destroying things and killing people.

I could have sworn I saw the bare branches lining the sidewalk down the block still moving like oars in and out of the wind as the breath of Roman galley slaves blew against my nostrils and the linings of my lungs.

And down the street the small neighborhood kids in the school playground's sandbox crawled like combat soldiers on their bellies up my nose.

MY THERAPIST'S PROCEDURE

The meds I take slow the steps I walk sweating the hour mile uphill to the Clinic and from the entrance to the door and then to a seat. My stomach's queasy. For the hundredth time, Dennis says nice things to me but I believe the opposite of what he says and I start acting desperate again. He asks me questions. He observes my body language and watches for the slightest change in expression around my eyes and at the edges of my mouth. Trying not to lie, I tell him the truth. Almost. He gets me to pretend my parents are seated in two empty chairs and me to say to them, "I'm sorry. I didn't know I was supposed to tell you anything. You never told me." They look stern and I start crying and my gut, stretched to the max, retracts like a rubber band. Resenting that my mouth and tongue feel so mushy, I hear my therapist's laughter. Then I feel my tears dripping into the slobber on my lips, and within seconds I see, through the water in my eyes, the images of my parents relax.

MY EARLY EDUCATION

John Wayne was the only man who ever reminded me of my father.
Dad was 6'4" tall when he was thirteen. With a boy's face and a
smaller knapsack he rode a freight into the Northwest and the Bull
onboard caught him by the shirttail and clubbed him a dozen times
with a baseball bat.

Dad was stubborn and still wanted to get to Seattle, so after two
bad days he moved his legs. Then he held his ribs together with his
hands and crawled out of a gully and back up into a boxcar headed for
the Pacific.

He joined the Civilian Conservation Corps, cleared trails and built
bridges in the Cascades, enlisted young in the Old Army's Signal
Corps and reenlisted in the New Army and hiked with malaria and
General MacArthur thousands of miles into New Guinea, the
Philippines and Japan.

And eight years after World War II, when Dad thought I had
learned how to listen and talk to people, he saw my mom taught me
my alphabet and how to read not just the comics but stories, too,
about poor folks and how we tried to live. Then he took me with him
into the wilderness where I learned how to be real quiet, start a
campfire and boil hobo coffee in a can.

THE LAST HUNDRED YARDS

I imagine him saying, "Will my kids inherit malaria, Doc?"
 "Rest," the doctor says. "Quinine, Nurse."

~~~

Burning seagulls dive into the sea. I see my dad holding another
man's head up out of the boiling water. The other man's a Japanese
pilot with long bandages wrapped around his eyes. Dad's swimming:
lifting his free arm and kicking his legs. A blanket of air bubbles
blinds him when the other man's weight forces him under and his
head broils like a large shrimp each time he bursts out of the flaming
water to breathe. For hours, now… for days, my dad's been exhaling
into the hot oily sea and inhaling the steam. He's thirsty.
Everything's shape changes into an explosion and incinerates the
wharves and pilings in his mind. The trees. The ships. The lives.
And, disobeying his President like the Japanese pilot his Emperor,
Dad pulls the Jap in with him to shore; and, still breathing, he hears
the wounded man moaning as the last of the man's bandages unravels
and lies between their bodies on the sand.

READING LITERATURE AGAIN

I'm not locked up now but I still can't face the outside world. I can't drive but some days I can walk before it gets hot to the tiny public library near downtown and read a few simple short poems in the local newspaper, a clearly written short-short story in a regional magazine or look at pictures in large old coffee table books about woodcarving, and trees, and other crafts and the great thinkers of Europe and Asia and writers, history and all the Fine Arts. I can read a little until I have to start over to remember what I read. It took me a month to read the first paragraph of Feodor Dostoevski's long novel *The Idiot*. It took me three months to read the first chapter... and now, after nine months, I'm where Prince Myshkin's having another mental breakdown and going back to the Swiss sanitarium... and I can't help thinking that I'm being warned that God's trying to tell me something.

Outside at home, at best, I scribble now, wandering around a yard or lost in a field. I think, talk and write in phrases, broken as fence rails busted off their posts... in words, heavy as rock chips blasted out of mountains that somehow were formed if not in my soul then in my heart.

My friends, blue collar workers and university professors, conservatives and anarchists, take me to the Little Theater in the Carpenters' Union Hall downtown and to the Olive Branch Bookstore near the train station to play guitar and sing my songs and read my poetry and prose from my chapbooks and journals after others and I have read passages from our favorite international authors out of spine-broken paperbacks from bookstores like Shakespeare & Co. in Paris and City Lights in San Francisco. I read aloud slowly the top words down to the words at the bottom on each hand-typed sheet of white typing paper I hold in my shaking hands. Shaking because I'm still afraid of being seen having such internal responses to everything... such immense feeling... such a drama inside me. And when I start to perspire I pretend Myshkin and Dostoevski are both standing at my elbows waiting to remind me to turn the page.

THE BLITZ OF ART
A Story

Roslyn was a real artist. She drew like a Renaissance master. I modeled for her off and on during the late 1960s; but after my illness she had a lot more to teach me than just how to paint portraits like Rembrandt or Norman Rockwell.

Six months after my breakdown we carried drawing supplies up to the San Luis Obispo train station. SLOooo-town was a garden. In every yard the edges of thousands of white citrus blossoms curled in the heat of the morning; and feeling warm, I inhaled the last of the cool air before I saw the old rust-colored engine that brought freight trains over the Grade and down into Grove and Arbor town, U.S.A.

The hot sun shining on the rust-colored engine reminded me Roslyn's husband Ed was delivering laundry to ranches where it was really hot up in the north county.

"You're sweating," Roslyn said as we got to the wood and stone benches out front.

I touched my wet head with my fingertips.

I kept thinking Roslyn knew more about being ill than I did; and maybe if I asked her she could tell me something that might help. But, then, maybe either she didn't, or it wouldn't. Or both.

"There's a washroom inside," she said.

"Some cold water, maybe."

I swallowed and tasted a few drops of my own sweat.

"Go ahead," she said, already marking the height and width of the water tank across the tracks on her paper. "Leave your things. I'll watch them."

~~~

I tried walking fast; but I was nearly out of breath.

I saw steam coming off the fences, the sidewalks and the rails around me like it once had off the dried old wood scaffolding that used to hold the buildings up. I thought of shotguns. I thought of dirt clods I had somewhere booted off the blade of a shovel. I remembered the smell of leather. I thought of the blazing coal furnaces on the steam engines of the late 1800s. I remembered my dad had been a hobo from the age of eleven to thirteen in the 1930s.

Approaching the station, I glanced at the chain fence on the other side of the tracks and thought about the barbed wire of concentration camps. I wiped my face with my shirtsleeve; and, seeing the gravel between and under the rails and ties near me, I imagined my dry gums were chewing my teeth.

~~~

I started seeing animated shapes in the mirror in the restroom. The shapes became darker as I looked deeper into the desperate look on my face.

I used a wet towel to wash my forehead and wrapped it around my wrists.

I closed my eyes and saw a light haloing the dark silhouette of a slim man and two small children. The shorter of the two curly-haired children bent her arm and jabbed the earth with the sharp edge of her hand trowel three times before she took a rest. The taller, a boy, reached for the handle of the shovel the man was leaning on. The three figures now looked like shadows moving behind a screen: visible but silent as I opened my eyes and saw the last of them fading out of sight in the mirror. The man had looked like an Okie digging the ground during the Depression.

~~~

It was Peter Barnes, I thought. A painter I knew a little. We had drawn together. I met him and his family in Berkeley the February before People's Park in May 1969. I helped them spade the ground to make an urban park and garden out of a bare lot that was only being used for a parking lot. Eventually it became a protest against the tyranny of local, state and federal authorities and therefore also the Vietnam War.

Pete. Katie. Teddy. And Lizzie.

I remembered a night Pete had stepped back from placing the light stand to the left of the model and began to establish the gesture of the figure with a reddish Conté crayon.

I looked at the model. Then I squinted my eyes and drew the large shapes of light and shadows in silence. Saving the smaller details for last, I drew how I felt in a long back-and-forth procedure. I drew the smaller and smaller forms of her body maybe in a state of awe until eventually I drew the puffy nipples on her breasts and the dead lashes extending from the thin pink lids of her extraordinarily beautiful eyes, delicately, by merely suggesting their presence.

~~~

Breathing normally again, I went outside.

Roslyn had stopped drawing the water tank and was just finishing gathering her sketchpad and small bag of assorted pencils into her arms.

"Was I gone too long?"

She looked at me carefully: at my face and eyes.

"No," she said finally. "Let's go into the cafe and get some coffee."

"Coffee… sure," I said.

"We can sit at a table and I'll draw you, or I'll draw the people inside."

"Okay," I said, hoping the place would be cool and empty.

~~~

I followed Roslyn into the Whistle Stop Cafe, staring at her long curly red hair and the light burnt sienna freckles on her face and arms. She led us down the aisle between four people at the counter and the three at a small table on our right to the farthest square table in the dark back corner. We sat in the shadows; and it took me a while to figure out if it was cooler or not.

It was; but I wasn't.

I counted again the seven other customers and the three older women who ran the cafe before I sank my elbow into the flat top of the wooden table; and, as I hid my warm damp face in my hand, I felt a log raft tilt nearly perpendicular to the sliding sandy floor of a river underneath my feet.

~~~

The three women weren't real handsome; but the two behind the counter were smiling and laughing and the one I saw through the window to the kitchen seemed to be cheerful whenever she sat food out and banged the small bell on the shelf between them.

I looked at how the two waitresses' light cotton dresses and aprons hung down over their huge stomachs, breasts and behinds.

"Mary and Joy are on the left at the counter and Gloria the one on the right's the cook today. They take turns cooking and serving," Roslyn said.

"Turns?" I said.

"They think it's fair, I suppose," Roslyn said.

I thought about my folks talking when I was a kid about taking turns and being fair. Remembering it, I felt comforted for a second.

Joy, the big tough-looking woman on the far left, finished pouring refills into the four guys' cups at the counter.

She's actually got a lit cigarette in her large soup bone looking hand, I thought. Where's the jukebox—the Country and Western? Old gal's singing Patsy Cline and blowing her smoke in their eyes and maybe knocking ashes off in their coffee. Poor me. Why me? Fair turns in misery.

Had any of these older people ever lost their minds though? Had they already taken years to get them back? Most likely not: was my answer.

The first pair of men at the counter looked like German or Swiss-Italian ranchers in white straw western hats, shirts and Wrangler jeans. The second pair wore identical charcoal-colored caps, long-sleeve plaid flannel shirts and black leather vests. They were smaller. They looked like Portuguese dairymen. The older looked grizzled. The younger seemed paler and thinner. He had a wimpy mustache, a higher voice and sounded sober.

~~~

"Your tractor driving ain't what it should be, either," the drunk older one said.

"No, Pa," the younger said.

"As a matter of fact," the older said, slobbering on the younger one's sleeve and shoulder, "you couldn't plow in a straight line if my life depended on it, could you? I stored ammunitions in New Guinea and the Philippines sweating from malaria. Mortars. Shells. Bombs. I held it. I carried it in my hands." He drooled.

The younger one faced the counter top and didn't move.

"The littlest of the five of us," the older man said, "he wasn't 4F. None of us were. He was bigger than me… and some Red left him on a hill in Korea."

"Coffee's hot, Tony," Joy told the older man. "And it's fresh."

"Hot as hell," the old man said. "Cold as hell. One move wrong… and my brother's dead."

"Yes, sir," the younger man said.

I imagined the son had tears in his eyes; and I wanted to get up and go over and hug him, to comfort him, but the light and shadows surrounding the two men and all the rest of us in the room seemed to thicken and the air for a moment seemed too heavy to move and I didn't dare move out of my seat.

~~~

The large waitress Mary wobbled toward us bringing a full sugar bowl with her.

"How you doing today, Roslyn?" Mary said, setting the sugar bowl down hard on the table. Her flabby arms shook from the impact, as well as her double chin and mashed potato looking hands.

"Fine. It's beautiful out," Roslyn said, and the two women smiled.

"Coffee?" Mary asked.

"Two coffees," Roslyn said. "Just two coffees."

"I'll bring you some cream, Dearie," Mary said, leaning toward us over the table. "You two stay as long as you like."

I stared at how wide and heavy Mary looked when she turned away.

~~~

"You able to drive, Tony?" Joy asked the older man at the counter.

"My name's Alberti," the man said, swinging his elbow nearly into the younger man's face.

Joy nodded. "We went to High School together, Anthony," she said.

"Ah, to hell with you. I'm going home," the older man said. Trying to stand up, he slouched and stumbled all over himself. He dropped a large green bill on the counter. Then he turned and slid like raw pancake batter off a large spoon back into a bowl.

The younger man reached for his father.

113

"I'm the one who works and pays the bills. I survived," his father said.

"That must be painful and embarrassing," Roslyn said.

"I see something like that and I'm glad mine's not around," I said before I realized Roslyn had already stopped talking.

~~~

I waited for the coffee, hoping the older man who had fallen back on his stool would stop being so loud.

Looking down at the table and the floor, I remembered my last pieces of art. First, the drawing of the guy spitting saliva out of his scraggly whiskered mouth as he stood in-between the cars trying to sell the Berkeley Barb to motorists stuck on Telegraph Avenue probably to earn enough money for his next tab of acid or bag of marijuana. Second, the wash drawing of the black U.C. coed grabbing her Afro while the helmeted riot cop beside her clubbed a Chicano student to the ground. And, third, the fully developed painting of the old woman as she turned in her seat to get up and off the College Avenue bus: the stern look, the deep wrinkles running like gullies in an awful-looking field, her shawl rolling over her bony shoulders, her ratty thin loose-fitting clothes, and the hair on her head extending like the bare branches of an October tree… like the teeth of a rake. Even the bristle curving out of a wart, or a mole, on her chin made her look like the ugliest grandmother of the accused young women at the Salem witch trials. Seeing the old woman last year had seemed nothing short of a warning. And my painting still looked like she was trying to warn me about something. I wondered again how beautiful she must have looked when she was young.

~~~

Roslyn looked at me like she was searching for something.

I shook my head.

"My mind changes now, Roslyn, like vapor… like my spirit dissipates like a cloud… like smoke. The sun gets too hot or a shadow covers my mind and my head hurts… and I feel like a dandelion in a harsh wind. And I'm falling apart."

Roslyn frowned.

114

"They could have locked me up for good if you two hadn't driven up and got me home. You were like medics coming in and getting me out. I wouldn't have made it, not in a mental hospital."

"Tell Eddie. He tried to be a medic during the Korean War but he has flat feet so he didn't pass the physical. They wouldn't let him be a soldier or a medic. He went to college later with Korean War vets he looked up to."

"Yeah... He probably did."

"Eddie's a very loyal person," Roslyn said. "And you're his best friend."

I thought about it for a second before I nodded.

~~~

I thought about how James Rector, the dead young black man at the People's Park riot, would never talk with his friends, his family or strangers again.

Mary brought a three-quarter full glass coffee pot to refill our cups. I stared at a gravy stain low on the shoulder strap of her large apron and then at the scalding hot coffee swirling in the pot as she reached to pour it. I saw it looked like something between dark oil and mud thickening as it settled.

Roslyn poured more of the cool cream into hers and added a teaspoon of sugar and stirred it with her stainless steel spoon which, then being wet, stained her folded paper napkin when she placed the spoon—right side up—down on it.

I remembered asking Pete, "Have you heard anything about Alan Blanchard?"

Pete's Conté crayon had hit the surface of his paper and exploded. Its red powder blasted his fingers and his face.

"Alan's blind," Pete yelled. "Just like the rest of us he'll never paint what he can't see. If he's lucky he can get into the Berkeley School for the Blind and learn Braille."

"Sorry, Pete," I had said. "I'm sorry."

I imagined seeing other guys being shot and blown apart. I thought about the bombing in Vietnam and the shooting.

I caught a glimpse of Roslyn while she was taking a sip of her cream-and-sugar-saturated coffee holding her cup in both hands.

115

Hearing laughter and seeing happy people were what I missed most in art museums, galleries and books… and in life, I thought, my attention returning slowly to the present. I had taken lots of photographs and drawn a lot of fast sketches to catch the smiles, the laughing faces and the looks of genuine happiness that are impossible for people to hold for even twenty minutes, much less for three hours. And children, of course, don't often pose for long at all. I thought about little Teddy and Lizzie.

~~~

I took the first sip of my second cup of coffee and started sweating again immediately.

Roslyn drew fast enough to draw children. We're all children. Roslyn drew from life; and I admired her drawings and paintings of people of all ages whether they looked happy or not.

Ed had told me about her emotional spells—but she hadn't. I had seen signs of her starting to become frustrated and desperate but never anything more than that. Roslyn painted, Ed talked and wrote. Ed and I must have liked arguing with each other because we talked and talked and talked.

I imagined Ed driving with his window down and burning his hands on the steering wheel up in the northern part of the county. He was short like the lines of his poems, and lean like crisp bacon frying on a rock in Mohave.

I knew his mind was busy working on something. I could see him wanting to reread Robert Frost or re-watch a John Wayne movie.

Ed needed America's actions to match her ideals; and he believed that they did so she didn't deserve to be criticized and he had a rationale and a rebuttal for every criticism I made. "We dropped the atomic bomb and we've got most of the missiles," I had told him, "but since we landed on the moon we're all children of the planet Earth… We're moved by the music. There're thousands of terrific bands. So maybe, just maybe, all the artists among us will help us see. No more winners and losers. No more contest."

~~~

Guys were shouting.

Roslyn started shaking her cup over the table.

116

The father at the counter flung his head over his shoulder, stood awkwardly and wobbled across the narrow space between us like he was a cougar hobbling drunkenly toward an endangered piece of meat. I could almost smell the dust on his face smoldering like ashes among the stumps of his two-day beard. I felt sweat drip off the ends of my eyelashes and cringed lower the closer he came. I saw his falling fists slam and depress the raw porous wood on the table and the glass jar of sugar shake and the salt-and-pepper shakers jump.

I felt the old man's hot breath bang me in the head like an orange-burning metal shovel being hurled heavy-handed out of a blacksmith's forge… and the singed nerves behind both of my eyes started to burn.

"You fucking hippie," the old man said.

Coming to—I looked him in his eyes.

"You raise hell and trash the country, you yellow chicken shits will face a flamethrower," the old man said. "Your feathers will stink up the sky."

His eyes reddened.

"If you weren't a bunch of babies still pissing your diapers I'd kill everyone of you I could find."

I clutched the edge of the table top with both hands hard; and I must have glared.

Enough young people—and babies—have been murdered, I thought, right? Or maybe I said it out loud…

~~~

"No fighting, Tony," Joy shouted from behind the counter.

"Not here," Mary added, huffing, charging toward us.

"Tony," Joy screamed as she slammed an empty cup solidly on the counter.

My knees shook.

The old man dropped his jaw; and his flushed face trembled. He must have heard the tone in Joy's voice or read my face, or Mary's or Roslyn's… or realized that he was greatly outnumbered.

He wobbled, turning left and right.

"We don't," he said, turning to me again. "We killed each other. Each other. That's what we did. I know what they're doing." He raised his fists like a prizefighter trying to defend his head and spun around like a limp red, white and blue flag falling over an entire planet of mass graves, military coffins and white crosses.

He was going down until his son caught him and held him up while half a million referees continued the count.

I kept my eyes on the back of his fat bright red neck as he was led away from me.

~~~

How much longer, I wondered as I leaned back in my seat.

I felt hot like a sun had slid out of the back of my own neck to my forehead and back… until I cooled like a cloud rising over the top of a rock this side of the moon. And then—holding my breath like a dandelion seed—I floated in space tumbling slowly forwards, sideways and backwards out among the broken down specks of meteors as the monochromatic underpainting of life turned into a rainbow… into colors… and I discerned the lost and found edges of yellow, red and blue shapes mixing as I awoke so slightly before I drowsily lowered my upper lids again and backed away into sleep like an underwater current submerging farther into the deep… as I drowned.

I reached for the sweat running diagonally across my forehead.

I glanced up again at the green eyes staring out of Roslyn's soft freckled face.

"What was yours like, Roslyn?"

"Not like him."

"Your being sick, I mean."

"Oh," she said. And then she paused for five seconds. "Mine were very conventional. My mother was a cold person," she said. "They sent me to doctors. I was diagnosed and medicated. I became delusional. I'd start screaming and not be able to stop. I remember my relatives—uncles, aunts and cousins—thought it was unfortunate what had happened to me but they seemed offended. There were more doctors. And electric shock… And teachers at art schools: good and bad… and the other students: good for me, and bad. Everything became difficult again. But Eddie wasn't frightened of me. The last time I got real sick I was put in Camarillo State Mental Hospital. The head doctor in charge of my case thought I needed to stop doing art altogether so I could keep in touch with reality. She had the staff take away anything they caught me drawing with, but I traded all my desserts for a tube of dark red lipstick and sketched on sheets of toilet paper and hid my sketches under mine and other patients' mattresses. I was in there for months."

I turned away from the haunted look in her face and looked down into the shadows under our table. I remembered seeing battles and demonstrations in movies and on the evening news... until she finally said, "One night Eddie jumped over a fence and helped me escape; and then, some time later, we came up here where he looks after me and I can paint..." and I looked up at the negative space around her green eyes and everything else in the room.

What are you looking at, Roslyn; and how do you see it, I wondered. Alan Blanchard's blind for the rest of his life; and James Rector's dead.

<center>~~~</center>

"When do you get your mind back?"

"Yours?" she said, giving me her honest look of not knowing. "In time, you can get help, and learn."

"Group," I said.

"Therapy, yes," she said. "Counseling."

I nodded a little and looked down again at her sketch and fingers.

"How we talk to ourselves. What to expect of others; and how to react."

"I want to be an artist," I said.

"You are." She said.

I looked past her hands and sketchpad lower into the shadows beyond us.

"Really," I asked, "how do you stand it?"

"It gets easier. I draw what I care about enough to look at," she said. "Sometimes I care and feel more. Things catch my eye and I try to look a little longer to see them whether they're a realistic image or an abstraction. And even after hundreds of large canvases now, I still try to be open, to stay sensitive and to grow... brushstroke to brushstroke... One day at a time. Don't the alcoholics say that?"

Roslyn glanced at the drunk at the counter; and then I did.

119

"Keep at it. You'll have to watch out for Eddie, though. He wants to mentor someone."

"And I'm it," I said, frowning before I smiled.

"It's obvious, isn't it?" she said. "He's been writing for years, but… "

"Other than a few readings he doesn't hang out with other writers," I interrupted.

"Eddie's very opinionated so he doesn't have many friends," she said.

~~~

"If you're not the one in the tractor seat doing the plowing, God help you," the drunk at the counter said, slobbering on his chin. "The Japs will come down the hill and stick you with a bayonet. The Chinks did."

"Okay, Tony," Joy said. "You've been carrying on long enough."

"What are you saying?"

"You heard," she said. Looking away, she took her last puff off the butt of her latest cigarette and blew the smoke down into the open trench she was standing in.

The young man was standing with his weight leaning on the counter: both arms extended toward his fingers stretched out between cups and plates in front of him.

"There," the old man shouted as he turned his red face to the left and slammed his large ring of rough-edged keys down hard.

"Take him home, Carl," Joy said, putting her cigarette out in a cheap metal ashtray between the dirty plates.

The younger man picked up the keys and slid them down into the small pocket on his vest.

"You ain't driving my truck—you ain't," the older man roared, turning his head to the right. "And I ain't saying I'm sorry to anybody. No one deserves it."

"And this," Joy said, handing the young man a paper napkin. "He's got steak and eggs on his mouth."

The younger man took the napkin and put it back down on the counter.

The old man looked half-befuddled trying to turn to his son. "You can't refuse your country," he said. "You can't do that. You can't be a hindrance or worthless."

"If they take me, Pa," Carl said.

"What?" the old man, Mr. Anthony Alberti, stopped turning back and forth. He slammed the weight on his shoulders against the younger man's rib cage and stomach. Then he slumped once again into his son's arms.

Pain has teeth, and the younger man was swallowing it. He had eaten enough that it was eating him inside out. So had his dad.

I watched the young man haul his dad out of the cafe.

"You okay?" Mary the waitress asked.

Roslyn added a darker value to one of the shadows in her drawing. Her shading looked fuzzy.

That man's hurting like I am, I thought.

Mary stood still for a second before she asked, "Can I get you anymore coffee?"

I was still staring at the drawing.

THE RIOT CLASS
A Story Of Berkeley

"It was not a confrontation," Carlos corrected Robert. "It was a slaughter."

The two young guys were eating dessert and drinking coffee in a small cafe on Telegraph Avenue near the entrance to the University of California at Berkeley. So far they'd been talking about students and poor people in Mexico and the United States.

Robert tried to look away from Carlos. He tried to look out the window but the sun shined too brightly through the gold sign letters on the glass. He also tried to swallow a mouthful of his apple pie and rum sauce and rid himself of his dirty fork at the same time but he missed the rim of his bowl and the fork fell on the table.

"They were trapped," Carlos said. "Five student leaders at the university got caught in an alley after they left a meeting on campus."

"The police shot them?" Robert finally asked.

"Yes, with machine guns. My sister knew one. She went to the hospital to visit him three days after it happened. He wasn't wounded as badly as the others, she told me. She saw him. It was horrible what the police did to them. One died. There was a large funeral procession. Thousands of students carried his body through the streets."

Robert imagined what Carlos was telling him before he said softly, "I didn't hear about it, Carlos."

"I found out about it from my sister. The newspapers here didn't report it," Carlos said.

Robert reached for his fork, but only held it near the surface of the table. The remains of apple pie, rum sauce and ice cream between his teeth and around his tongue tasted sickening sweet. He shook his head.

"The students in your country involve themselves very seriously in your country's politics," he said.

"Yes, they do. One day they will in yours, too. Maybe soon here in Berkeley."

Robert's head hurt: bad.

He lowered his fork into the bowl. The tines sank quickly through the last of the ice cream and rum sauce all melted and swirled together at the bottom. The aftertaste of the dessert had tasted bitter. There was a sharp pain as if the ends of the tines were internally piercing his stomach.

~~~

Three months later, Robert went to see Carlos at a Third World Liberation Front picket line on campus near Sather Gate. He got there just before the three campus cops.

The shortest cop put his hands on his hips and cocked his head back and showed his teeth. "Come here," he said to the young black reporter. Then he turned to the small crowd of mostly black students. "All right, people. You guys with picket signs got five seconds to get them and yourselves out of here."

"Five seconds?" the reporter shouted.

"I told you to get out of that line," the short cop said. He leaped toward the reporter, grabbed him around the neck and pulled his head down against his hip.

"What're you doing, Pig?" one of the black students shouted.

"What's he done?" Carlos shouted louder than everyone else.

"Obstructing entry to this campus and resisting arrest."

"No, he's not," Carlos yelled.

The reporter twisted his body to free himself and shriveled up his face. White saliva bubbled on his lips as he raised his head trying to catch his breath.

Carlos banged the cop in the shoulder to force him to release the reporter but it didn't work.

"They're killing him," screamed a coed beside Robert. "My God, do something."

The two tall cops grabbed the reporter by his arms and started pulling on him. The short cop let go of the guy but stayed behind him and then rose up and came down slugging him in the back of the neck with his fist.

Ten yards to the right of Carlos, Robert stood there watching.

~~~

The next day, Robert woke up more confused than usual. Then it hit him. He was supposed to join Carlos and others for a serious student strike on campus. He promised.

Eventually, he wiped the sleepers out of his eyes. He got up off the mattress on the floor. He gathered his scattered clothes from the shadows in the room. Then he put on his light blue work shirt and rolled the long sleeves up over his elbows while he walked into his kitchen and faced the sunlight entering the window.

He could handle joining Carlos on a picket line, he thought, or at a small demonstration. He could if it was nonviolent. Today, he could.

He turned away from the warm light and stepped through the cool dark hallway to the door. In the outer hall, he locked his door and turned toward the wooden stairs. He reached for the handrail, combed back his hair with his fingers and started his rapid footwork, skip and a shuffle down the steps.

"And a hard, hard rain's a-gonna fall." Dylan.

Today wasn't yesterday, Robert reminded himself. Whatever happened would be different. He was just excited.

"Are you experienced?" Jimmy Hendrix.

~~~

Robert slowed down when he reached Durant and Telegraph Avenue. He rubbed his face to wipe the last of the crusty sleepers out of his eyes and turned left toward campus.

He felt light-headed.

Traffic was bumper to bumper in the street and both sidewalks were crowded. His first thirty steps, shoppers and students from all five continents and the local panhandlers representing their own international class were all present and visible. Two record stores with outdoor speakers blasted Janis Joplin and The Dead; the open door of the bookstore Shakespeare & Co. looked inviting; and Moe's and Cody's held anything else you would want if you really wanted to follow Grace Slick and The Jefferson Airplane's directive to "feed your head."

Sunlight shined off the windows. He stared into one and saw his face on the glass. Something about him going to a protest demonstration now seemed artificial and dangerous.

He shoved his hands deep into his pockets, looked up and tried to put his anxious feelings into the white clouds passing across the endless blue sky far beyond the tops of the buildings on the other side of the street and up ahead on campus but his feelings stayed way down inside him.

He would be with a friend, he thought. And maybe someday he would be more like him.

He felt a lot of things because he thought too much.

~~~

Robert speeded up the last block toward campus.

Crazy Billy bobbed out of the waves of people on the sidewalk. Billy had long light-brown hair and a short thin mustache and beard. He also had acne and was grinning so much Robert could see the white puffy remains of Billy's last carbohydrate meal wedged between his teeth.

"Guy's talking like he's Billy Graham holding the Ten Commandments over their heads," Billy said loudly.

Robert walked on, but the shorter Billy tagged along beside him. Billy chuckled.

"I'm gonna get out of here," Billy said, "and go live with real monkeys. Real ones live wild in the jungles in Africa. Hey! They got monkeys in Vietnam. All these guys like from High School are out there with flamethrowers frying monkeys out of trees, Man."

Robert felt Billy's warm breath.

Out of my tree, Billy.

Robert stepped back into the old baker who was carrying some repair tools out to the ladder in front of the Apple Pie Cafe. Caught off-balance, the pock-faced baker held on to the ladder but he dropped a hammer. The good-sized hammer hit and flew three or four feet toward Billy.

"Wow," Billy said, picking up the hammer out in front of him. "Here's your hammer." He laughed. "You better put everything you got in your pocket and drive nails through it. Like this."

Billy demonstrated in the air how to drive a nail all the way in with a single swing.

"Nail your head to a stone in a cemetery," he said. "Like this, see?"

He struck the air again.

128

"Wham! You got a fallout shelter down in the basement? Go get it. Take this hammer with you, get inside it and lock yourself in. Nail your shoulder to the door."

Billy lowered the hammer. He squat down and shoved the hammer back toward the foot of the ladder.

"There's your hammer."

The old pockmarked baker stooped and reached. He yanked the hammer and came up threatening to hit Billy.

"Do it quiet," Billy said. He giggled and looked back over his shoulder toward campus. "You're not as tough as Grandpa."

"Delinquent!"

"He didn't bump you, sir," Robert said. "He's not well."

"I'm not the one who's sick," Billy laughed. "Just wait, man. Old Grandpa's lacing his boots up in the basement."

"Look, Mister," Robert said. "It's crowded out here, right? I did it. It was an accident."

"College brats," the baker said. "Drug addicts!"

Robert turned his back toward the old man. He glanced at the sidewalk and saw people's shoes, feet and sandals. Why do old people always stick up for the System? He wondered. Scared, he guessed. Frightened lost sheep even in a flock, he thought. And then he admitted to himself that he wasn't much of a wolf, or even a sheepdog either.

Robert looked up at the faces around him. He was also easily embarrassed, he realized, and afraid of not looking normal.

Crazy Billy had split.

~~~

Robert walked through the students on the Student Union steps. He looked out over the huge crowd in Sproul Plaza and tried to see Carlos but sunlight reflecting off the Administration building glass windows blinded him a bit. He only saw glimpses of the backs of heads and a few faces of kids he didn't recognize.

Carlos will be somewhere at the front, Robert thought.

He looked again at the thousands of students. He saw pockets in the crowd, but not many. He would have to veer one way and then another to get through it. He could bump a lot of people and a lot of people just might bump him back.

How did people ever find their friends, he wondered, at the demonstrations last year in Munich and Berlin?

The flames of the German students' bonfires had risen and swirled among their flags and banners as the students gathered in the streets and stadiums to protest the real values and actual practices of their government and the governments of the U.S.S.R. and the United States. Those heroic students liberated slogans from the minds and books of intellectuals, painted them on the walls of libraries and shouted them in public for everyone else in the world to see and hear.

~~~

Robert stopped. He was daydreaming, so he went back to scanning the backs of students' heads.

A thin guy wearing a tan corduroy sport coat stood at a portable microphone stand on the Sproul Hall steps. He jerked his head around and lashed his forehead with his blond hair. He rolled off the mic and then thrust his mouth back on it.

"The black student strikers and their supporters were forced to remove their placards and themselves from the entrance to this campus," he said. "The cops arrested the black reporter Richard Carver and dragged him off. The Free Speech Movement was four years ago. What are the cops doing on this campus?"

"End police harassment," a student shouted.

Warm sunlight ricocheted off the planes and edges of the Sproul Hall steps.

"There's a riot squad, right now, downstairs in the basement under Sproul Hall," the thin speaker in the tan corduroy sport coat said. "The corporate imperialists who run this country still want to control our options and regulate our dissent. As long as they hold the power... as long as law and order supports their self-interest they claim we have democracy and freedom. Police and military intervention: that's their tradition, and that's the System."

"Eldridge Cleaver for President!" someone shouted.

Two or three people laughed loudly.

"Free Bobby Seale!" someone screamed.

"Black Panthers, yes! The cops in Oakland, no!" someone yelled. There. There he is.

Robert saw Carlos running out of the front of the crowd and skipping up the Sproul Hall steps to the speaker on the mic. His dark hair and thin Spanish build: a politically conscious Mexican architect student.

The speaker stepped back from the microphone.

Carlos held a note up in his hand and waved it while he leaned into the mic and said, "Student Council's just voted in favor of a strike. I'd like to remind everyone the campus paper came out in favor of the strike this morning, and the Faculty Committee did so late last night. This campus is officially closed."

The blond speaker flexed his legs and arms and jerked his head back. He raised and pounded both of his fists in the air. "You've got a strike on campus, Chancellor," he shouted into the mic. "You've got a strike!"

The crowd cheered.

Robert smiled but he smeared the few streams of sweat starting to run down his forehead. Then he pressed his fingertips into the sweat. He was not a leader. He never had been. He was afraid of crowds. He was scared of the authorities. At best, he was a sidekick and not a good one. And yet, he still wanted to be like the earlier Berkeley Free Speech Movement student leader Mario Savio… or Bob Dylan. But he had never faced a policeman much less stood in the way of a riot squad. So, what if this protest led to something even more serious and he wasn't brave or smart enough to cope with it?

Robert stepped back. He watched a shadow spread across the step toward the toes of his unpolished brown shoes. He backed up, turned around and watched himself walking away, thinking he was a coward and feeling miserable.

~~~

Fifteen minutes later, Robert sat below old football team photographs hanging on the walls of a booth in the Bears' Den at the rear of the first floor of the Student Union. The photographs blurred. Dots of ink swirled under the glass between the frames.

He raised his hand and rubbed his head. He felt weak and scared.

He sipped his coffee.

No books, he thought. This was strange. He always hauled his books around. He read books nearly all day. He turned page after page, underlining phrases and paragraphs.

Do the research. Write papers. Know how everything relates. Inter-relates. How things are similar. How they're different. Be objective but remain true to the uniqueness of your own perspective. Perhaps you'll gather relevant information and recognize what is significant and formulate an original idea to shed light on the dark massive picture of current events for someone who needs to make a decision that will affect the future of the world and the lives of everyone in it. That would be something. It would make all the struggling worthwhile. Read.

But today he hadn't read anything yet.

Looking around, he only recognized one of the other students in the room: his neighbor Marie Johnson. She was sitting and talking with a guy at a near table.

She was a small, determined coed, he thought... a black princess of the Social Sciences, Humanities and Liberal Arts of the New York City school system. He had talked to her enough times to have a heart-to-heart, or two.

She and the white guy she was with were arguing.

"Bad idea, Marie."

"A student strike," she said.

"Stop classes and guys will lose their deferments. We'll be drafted," the guy said.

"Half of Queens—and half the young black men on the East Coast —have been drafted," she said.

"So?" the guy demanded. "What do you mean?"

"I'm going back out there," she said.

Other people in the room started shouting.

A muscular guy burst into the room yelling, "Riot squad!"

A short coed entered behind the guy and yelled, "They're using tear gas. It's coming into the building."

A thin guy behind her screamed, "Everybody out! They're clubbing people! They're chasing us off campus!"

"If they want to have their heads bashed in—or blown out—let 'em," the guy with Marie said. "I value my intelligence. I wouldn't give the bastards the satisfaction."

Marie stiffened. Then she scooted her chair back, got up and left the room.

Robert noticed he was holding his coffee cup hard in the palm of his hand like the centers and quarterbacks holding footballs in the photographs on the walls.

~~~

Seven minutes later, Robert slid his head down the cold smooth face of the front glass wall of the Student Union. Tear gas clouds covered the entire plaza; and filled the Student Union lobby. The gas tasted acrid.

He stared at the last half-dozen stragglers still running around outside. One was trying to get up out of the water fountain on the left to escape a riot cop wielding a club. Water poured off his clothes. He leaped out of the fountain.

"Move," Robert thought.

His eyes burned bad. His lips quivered. Something tasted green. He was going to vomit. He shook his head and swerved around holding one of his arms over his stomach.

A dark-haired guy ran through the center of the lobby.

A coed pressed her long straight hair tightly against the sides of her tear-stained face with the open palms of her hands. She was shaking. "They're gassing us," she shouted. "They're policemen. My eyes burn. My eyes are burning." She rubbed her face with the backs of her hands. "No one can go out there!" she shouted. "I can't go outside! Why are they doing this?"

Then she walked away into the light streaking through the rear glass wall.

Robert listened to the echo of her shoes hammering the floor.

He dropped his head into his hands. He doubled over and started coughing from deep inside his chest. Saliva hit and splattered against the inside of his lips and teeth.

Lifting his head, he looked through the sunlight shining through the gas, trying to focus on the rear glass wall. He saw students running out the backdoor. Bobbing his head, he stumbled after the last of them. He tried to stop coughing but he couldn't.

~~~

Out back, he leaned against the waist-high wall and breathed rapidly.

His eyes still burned but he tried to focus on the few white clouds in the sky far off beyond the East Bay and San Francisco.

He remembered how much he liked to feel a morning mist tickling his cold cheeks in the High Sierras.

He wondered about the bombing and fighting happening at that very moment in Vietnam… how many young men were shooting at someone, and how many were being shot at… and how many farmers' families would prefer to have their eyes burn from tear gas than to have their whole bodies burn from napalm?

He looked right and saw that the Westside of campus was clear of tear gas and cops, so he still had a way to escape. Feeling safer, he looked left and… there. He saw Carlos standing in a small crowd of students and street people surrounding a police van parked on Bancroft Way, the first block west of Telegraph Avenue.

~~~

This smaller crowd was wedged into a narrower space. Robert led with his head and pushed forward. A guy nearly hit him in the mouth with his elbow. Robert raised his arm and held it like a shield to wedge his way farther in.

"Wait a… Hey," a coed whined, tossing her long hair toward him as she turned to see who was pushing past her. Robert smelled the warm scent of her recently shampooed hair. He squinted. Then he realized he was starting to sweat again.

He saw the small red "Campus Books" sign high in the glass window behind Carlos and the students huddling around the police van. Used books. Had he read too many, or not enough? He shook his head and bumped another guy.

People were pushing on the police van.

"Push harder," one shouted.

"Don't!" Carlos yelled.

134

Robert continued sweating as he crossed the street. He felt light-headed. A dozen or more students were rocking the van, trying to topple it on its side.

Robert tapped Carlos on the shoulder and stepped between him and the people backing away from the van.

Carlos grabbed Robert's shoulder.

"Get back," he shouted. "Get out of the way."

People screamed.

The hollow van made a loud thud sound when it hit the street. The sound, Robert thought, was as wide and as high as the roar of a full-grown male lion swallowing everything within a mile of it.

People cheered.

Robert pulled his arms through the sweat on his forehead until his rolled up sleeves were drenched. Then he re-opened his eyes.

The police van roof now stood like a wall, perpendicular to the street: a bare wall primed for a mural or graffiti in a Central or South American town.

"There's nobody in it. Hit it," one guy shouted.

Three students climbed up on the van's side and at least two groups of up to half-a-dozen others started pounding on the van with their bare fists and kicking it with their feet.

Carlos put his arm around Robert's shoulder.

"You're sweating," he said.

Robert wrapped his wet arm around the back of Carlos's waist. He grabbed the far side of Carlos's shirt and held on tight. Robert felt the dampness of his clothes against his body. He tried to focus through the sweat in his eyes and to slow his breathing. He felt sweat dripping off his nose.

A big student standing near the van's windshield held one of the torn-off large side mirrors. He raised the mirror over his shoulder, clenched his teeth and stared at the cracked glass in the windshield.

"The cops have had their riot. Now, we'll have ours," a smaller guy shouted. "Throw it."

"Death to the Fascists."

"Do it, do it, do it now," several of the students chanted.

The big guy with the mirror hurled it through the windshield. Glass shattered and crumbled into little pieces: some into the cab, and some outward to the ground.

The big guy looked at the broken glass glistening above the dark grime of the pavement. He looked pleased and proud of himself. He smiled.

Carlos dropped his arm.

"This isn't going to help, is it?" Robert said.

Carlos shook his head.

"Minority student leaders organized a peaceful demonstration. The police charged in and turned it into a riot."

Robert breathed.

"We've got to get back on campus," Carlos said, "and somebody's got to lead this." He pointed toward the gas clouds at the end of the block: the intersection between Telegraph Avenue and the mouth to campus.

"Coming?" he asked.

Robert took another breath and nodded.

~~~

People ahead of them had left the street and were hugging the buildings along the sidewalk.

Robert caught himself staring down at their legs moving through the shadows between them. He was finally going to stand up with Carlos against the authorities, he thought.

He remembered the students at the *May Night of the Barricades* last year in France: the sixty thousand students who closed down the universities of Paris and barricaded streets with bricks and rubbish— garbage cans, burned cars and uprooted trees—stacked in piles every eighty or a hundred feet. Tear gas rose through the smoke of fires raging in eight story buildings while thousands of France's riot police slowly hobbled down the streets wielding billy clubs and metal shields over the debris. Unraveled water hoses lined the pavement. Power is in the street, not in Parliament. *La Societe Est Une Fleur Carnivore.* Society is a carnivorous flower—the French poet Baudelaire. Students cursed. They sang. They faced their parents, and said no to their nation's police like students in the United States had done at the National Democratic Convention in Chicago, at the Pentagon back east and at the van down the block.

Gusts of tear gas filled Robert's nostrils and his lungs.

Maybe getting in the way, and staying there, was the exact thing he and everyone else needed to do, he thought.

"I need to get by," Carlos said to someone.

"What's his problem?" someone else said.

"Hold it," someone said.

Students shouted and drivers trapped in their cars half-a-block or more away pounded on their horns.

A dozen riot cops swung their clubs charging down the street toward the kids still demolishing the police van. Four dozen other cops crossed through a hundred students wandering around in the gas in the intersection. The cops started jabbing people. A frizzy-haired guy jumped up and down, pulling on a cop's gas mask. A black student lunged toward a cop's back and hit him on his shoulder blades with her fists. The cop turned around, striking her automatically across her breasts and face with the fist-end of his club.

Robert doubled over. He grabbed his stomach. He felt the pain in his forehead move toward the back of his head. He spun in circles, trying to grab on to something so he would not fall.

Tears wet his cheeks.

He could not see Carlos.

He felt the hard flatness of the pavement under his shoes and something like the coarseness of a hefty paper bag against his knuckles. Then he saw the elderly woman next to him holding a large shopping bag from her forearm. She was pounding on the glass door of the building behind him.

"You had it open just a minute ago," she shouted, leaning the side of her face against the glass. "I saw you. You're in there," she whimpered, pounding louder on the door. "I know you're in there."

Robert grabbed the edge of the doorframe and tried to breathe. But he couldn't.

~~~

Robert sat on the wood floor up against a wall in the Apple Pie Cafe. The old baker stood on his right and the elderly woman from outside now sat on the short bench on his left. The old woman was clutching an embroidered handkerchief to her eyes. Other people sat at small tables in the center of the room or stood rising into the shadows farther inside the cafe.

The old baker leaned against the glass entrance door with his shoulder and held on to the knob.

The blunt noise of the crowd outside kept hitting the building like a battering ram.

Robert raised his elbows to his knees and lowered his face to his hands. When he noticed he was shaking, he grabbed the back of his calves and rammed his tailbone farther back into the angle between the wall and the floor.

He saw the elderly woman lower her embroidered handkerchief away from her eyes. She was still sobbing.

"Keep drying your eyes, m'am," the guy on the other side of her said. "Your tears will only make the burning worse."

"Oh," she said, sniffling, and shutting her eyes.

"He's a doctor," the next guy said.

Crazy Billy stood leaning back against the wall shaking his head. "It's a bad trip."

"You don't look like a doctor," the woman said to the guy next to her.

"He's not wearing his uniform, Lady," Crazy Billy said.

"I work at the Student Health Center," the guy said.

"Yeah. He's got to intern either in Africa or here on Telegraph Avenue." Billy wrinkled up his light-hairy face and laughed. "Africa."

"Just breathe normally, m'am. You're going to be all-right," the guy said.

"A doctor with long hair and a thin mustache," she said.

"No, a medic. Yes, m'am."

Robert felt the old baker turning toward him.

"You again," the baker said.

Robert looked up at him and saw he was looking at Billy.

Billy laughed again.

"I just replaced a window last week," the old baker said. "These windows aren't cheap. Work hard somewhere safe and decent, you'd think you would be... You young people have no respect for the authorities, or anybody. I want you out of here."

"Sir," the medic said, standing up fast. "There's a riot."

The old baker glared at him.

Robert put his hands flat on the floor and pushed himself up.

"You're nuts," Billy said. "Tear gas's bad for my acne, man."

The baker slid back the bolt on the door and opened it. He pointed to the doorway. "All of you out. Now."

"All-right," the medic said.

Billy followed the medic into the fresh tear gas billowing into the cafe. Robert followed Billy. He glanced at the baker when he passed him and the man cringed. His old eyes blinked rapidly and his skinny lips shook.

"Out," the baker said.

Robert nodded and kept on going.

"Close the door," the old woman now behind them shouted from the bench.

~~~

Robert thought they were stepping into the fresh tear gas outside like three filled coffins being lowered next to each other in the ground as he saw the circle of cops in front of campus on his left and felt the burning in his eyes coming back. Gas spiraled and swirled.

"Hurt them," screamed a coed charging off the far corner, "hurt them bad." Her long auburn hair bounced off a cop's body as she hurled herself against him. The side of her face hit his visor. The cop pushed her away, knocked her to her knees and hit her half-a-dozen times in the stomach with the blunt end of his club.

People screamed, "Kill the Pigs."

Billy started running up the sidewalk toward campus. Robert took two or three steps after him and stopped. Billy was way too fast.

They'll hurt him, he thought.

Robert and the medic guy watched Billy's unprotected back until he disappeared among the cops and students near campus and Robert rubbed his eyes again and made the burning worse.

"I'm going down to the opposite corner," the medic said and pointed to the right.

Cops were pushing shouting and screaming students back through the intersection a block south of campus. Students rammed their shoulders into the people behind them. Two or three students fell backward out of the side of the crowd and a lot of other people backed up over their legs.

Robert stared now at the riot cops' white helmets.

Governor Reagan and the cops, he thought, were getting paid to do this.

"Come on," the medic guy said. "Stay on the sidewalk if you're coming."

~~~

Carlos faced the thousand students out in the middle of the street; and the wall of riot cops behind him stared at his back. The nearest cop raised a riot club parallel to the pavement.

"Back to campus," Carlos shouted while he backed up half-a-dozen steps shaking his fist in the air over his head. "Sproul Plaza. All of us together."

Carlos turned around as the cop behind him raised his club over his helmet and swung it like a hammer to nail Carlos six feet deep into the ground. The cop struck him at the base of his neck.

The cop raised his club again, grabbed Carlos by the shirt and started shaking and spinning him around in front of the crowd.

Carlos doubled over at the waist before he pulled free and fell. He hit the street with his shoulder and the back of his head. He gritted his teeth, screamed and rolled over on his belly. Then he groaned and dropped his face to the ground.

Pain shot through Robert's forehead. Heat rushed through his body but something cold chilled his heart.

The riot cop hit Carlos across the back of his legs. Then he hit him again.

Robert felt the cold inside him fall toward the pavement when he stepped off the curb.

The cop swung his club across Carlos's back.

Carlos shriveled up his face like a person having convulsions. He punched the air between his mouth and the pavement with his breath.

The cop crouched over him and raised his club back over his shoulder.

Robert grabbed the middle of the cop's club and pulled it toward him and then down over his hip. He twisted it so hard with both of his hands it flew out of the cop's fist.

The riot cop fell backward. His shoulder hit the pavement. Then his helmet did.

Robert spun around and swung the club back over his shoulder. He glared at the plastic visor on the cop's helmet.

Robert sensed the crowd coming toward him.

Several people bumped the sides of his back. The crowd was advancing all around him.

"Kill the Pigs!" one of the students shouted.

Robert loosened his grip on the solid club and dropped it. He stepped back, turned around and moved toward Carlos.

Half-a-dozen students tripped over Carlos before he got to him, knelt down and turned him over.

"Any sharp pain, Carlos?"

Carlos shook his head. "It burns," he moaned.

"Where?"

"Across my shoulder, my back and the back of my legs."

Robert grabbed Carlos's hand. He put his arm underneath Carlos's back. "Help me get you up."

Carlos opened and shut his eyes.

Robert pulled Carlos's arm up over his shoulders and around his neck. He stood up, bent over under Carlos's weight.

People banged into Robert's back.

"Can you walk?"

"It hurts," Carlos said.

He was gritting his teeth again.

Robert got Carlos up and walked him toward the curb. He stepped up on the curb. Then he pulled Carlos up into the smaller crowd on the corner. He bumped a lot of people real hard.

~~~

"Down," Carlos said, reaching for the sidewalk with his hand. "I've got to sit down."

Robert stepped beyond the small crowd on the corner and back off the sidewalk. He let Carlos's legs slide out into the empty cross street. Carlos followed Robert to the curb and landed with his head and shoulders in Robert's lap.

"It burns," Carlos whispered.

Tiny blisters of sweat sparkled in Carlos's hair. He slipped his arm over the outside of Robert's knee and pulled it toward him.

The student medic from the Apple Pie Cafe came up, reached down and placed his hand against the back of Carlos's neck.

"Can you help him?" Robert asked.

The longhaired medic ran his hand up and down Carlos's spine. Then he raised Carlos's head. He used his thumbs and fingers to open Carlos's eyelids and looked into his eyes.

"Get him to Emergency to be safe," the medic said.

"He lives near Alta Bates Hospital," Robert said.

"X-rays," the medic said as he stood and walked back to coughing and crying people nearer the building.

"Where are the police?" Carlos asked.

Robert looked through the gas at the riot cops swinging their clubs at people. The students were backing up again.

"Bunching the crowd up in the intersection," he said.

"We're too far off campus," Carlos said. "We had everyone united. I thought we had the leadership." He raised his hand, waved it in the air and dropped it. He grabbed Robert's knee for support. He pushed down on it, got his legs back underneath him and slowly stood up. "Nothing more can come of this. I'm leaving."

He bent his knee way too much when he took his first step and nearly fell.

"Can you walk?" Robert asked.

Not well, he couldn't... but they walked west and then south toward Carlos's apartment near the Oakland-Berkeley border.

Streets were deserted.

Carlos absolutely refused to go to Alta Bates Hospital so they kept on walking down the last block to his place. At the top of the short steps, Robert grabbed the doorknob and turned it.

"What will happen, Carlos?"

"Minority students must lead this strike. We need the white majority to understand that. We need to be nonviolent, and aggressive. We'll plan something. In an hour or two we'll be on the phone and stay on it all night."

Carlos pushed the door open ahead of Robert and limped inside.

~~~

Robert got home about 8 p.m. and went upstairs to the roof.

He had stayed at Carlos's place while Carlos soaked in a tub of hot water. He made a pot of coffee while Carlos started phoning his friends to come over. They were white, black and Hispanic and they were all experienced activists.

He now leaned against the short wall on the edge of the roof and looked through the dark across the bridge and over the water toward the lights of San Francisco. He thought the lights shined like beacons guiding planes full of people from all around the world.

He breathed.

But tear gas still burned in his mind. Black and white everything merged into gray. He felt like he was taking another test. This one felt like a final. A big one like his life depended on it.

Would he read about people suffering for the rest of his life and never do anything to stop it? Or would he stop reading, stay home and stare vicariously at some fantasy on television?

Robert felt like crying, but he couldn't.

He thought he would never know for certain whether or not the light he saw by was leading him in the right direction. For a moment he thought he was blind, and he felt lost.

~~~

The next morning Sproul Plaza looked better.

Three-hundred mostly minority professors, teaching assistants and undergraduates paraded in the plaza. They walked in an oval, carrying flags and banners. Carlos marched with a limp near the front. Robert thought the marchers looked more triumphant each step they took. Marching empowered them. Lap after lap. Their spirit rose and their pace increased.

Marie tapped him on his shoulder.

"You here?" she said, acting glad to see him.

"To support a friend," Robert said, and gestured toward the marchers.

"Me, too." she said. "Things I read in the papers really upset me sometimes."

"What's that?" he asked.

"This redneck Sheriff captain who got his picture in *The Chronicle*, holding his arm in a sling with a big grin on his face, said he got hit in the arm by a rock as big as a boulder. Guy's grinning and laughing about the whole thing." She raised her voice. "Where'd anybody find a boulder on campus? I'd like to meet the coed who picked a boulder up and threw it at this man."

Robert smiled.

"This captain said he's been to all the Bay Area demonstrations. Said the riot yesterday was the worst. Said his men did a good job stopping it."

"You a feminist, Marie?"

Marie shook her head. "I'm a strong young black woman from Queens."

Robert nodded, and they both laughed.

~~~

The parade started to break apart.

The head of the line headed out of the plaza through Sather Gate and the rest followed. Only the tail of the line still had to finish most of their last lap.

Robert and Marie joined the end of the line and marched out through Sather Gate. Maybe fifty students with black armbands walked along the line to monitor and encourage everyone to be calm and peaceful. This group of demonstrators were policing themselves, Robert thought. Their united presence and silence would be their strength.

They walked on past Dwinelle Hall.

Another hundred yards and they sat down on the grass lawn facing the University Avenue entrance to campus. Carlos sat with three or four of his activist buddies up at the front. Marie sat with some friends of hers. Robert stood by himself for a moment in the middle of the seated crowd before he went up and sat down in the empty space on Carlos's right.

Carlos looked up and smiled. They both leaned toward each other. Carlos stared into Robert's eyes.

Robert moved his finger through the grass and breathed more of the fresh morning air.

"Cómo estás?" he asked.

"Bien."

Robert watched the sunlight shining off the glass and steel-beam walls of the multi-story building across the street. He stared at the dark bulky shapes of the elite San Francisco Tactical Squad positioned on the roofs and along the grounds. Some thirty or more specially trained and heavily armed riot cops were guarding Governor Reagan and the rest of the U.C. Board of Regents while they met inside to decide what to do about the strike. The California VIPs had something to protect, Robert thought, and today it was us who they thought they had to defend it from.

Robert felt the warmth of the sunlight and the coolness of the grass on his fingers. He looked at the other students around him. He rubbed his hands on the lawn. He looked up at the clear blue sky and breathed.

He had taken a hard test, and passed it. And was about to start another. He raised his palms to the sunlight.

He was here, he thought, and let his hands drop to the lawn.

Carlos cringed as he raised his hand and squeezed Robert's shoulder. "Thank you, Robert, for pulling me out of the street before that cop killed me."

"You're welcome," Robert said.

"Oh, Robert," Carlos said. "Look at all these beautiful people."

And Robert did, and nodded.

He felt wonderful.

Author:

Don Wallis was born in 1946 in San Luis Obispo, California.
Raised in the northern San Joaquin Valley, he performed his
conscientious objector alternative service in Berkeley during the
Vietnam War, studied Intellectual & Cultural History of the Modern
World, Literature and Theater Arts at Cuesta College, Cal Poly State
University and University of California, Santa Barbara, and acted in
100 roles on stage and radio before starting his 30 year career as a
puppeteer. A spokesman for children, mental health and social
change, Don has been a poet, playwright, prose writer and an artist
for fifty years. He lives in San Luis Obispo. His website is
www.donwallis.com.

www.ingramcontent.com/pod-product-compliance
Lightning Source LLC
Chambersburg PA
CBHW030517260626
47157CB00005B/1779